CAMERA AT SEA

CAMERA AT SEA

THE HISTORY OF THE ROYAL NAVAL PHOTOGRAPHIC BRANCH 1919–1998

NEIL MERCER

Airlife

England

Dedication. For Tracey and Joseph David Mercer.

Note. This publication contains 'an impassioned plea for the retention of the Royal Naval Photographic Branch which is, in part, quite damning and subjective' (MoD(N) clearance letter 24/03/98). Clearly none of the opinions expressed therefore reflect the position of the Royal Navy or the Ministry of Defence (Navy), and should be interpreted solely as belonging to the author.

Photographs and Copyright. The images in this book have been obtained from a variety of sources, and have all been deemed Crown Copyright for the purposes of reproduction fees – and paid for. This blanket assumption is in no way intended to infringe copyright of individuals where it has been morally asserted.

British Library Cataloguing-in-Publication Data
A catalogue record for this book
is available from the British Library

ISBN 1 85310 889 8

Typeset by Servis Filmsetting Limited
Printed in Hong Kong

Airlife Publishing Ltd
101 Longden Road, Shrewsbury SY3 9EB, England
Telephone: 01743 235651 Fax: 01743 232944
E-mail: airlife@airlifebooks.com

CONTENTS

ACKNOWLEDGEMENTS

This account has been extremely difficult to research and assemble, hampered both by the wanton destruction of material in the 1980s and the internecine warfare which continues to fatally damage the Branch to this day. The project was assembled without the authority, knowledge or help of particular elements, whose attitude epitomises why the Photographic Branch is now under such significant threat. They know who they are.

'Tracey Barrett of Weymouth lived with me and helped me throughout the preparation of this book, both with support and looking after my son during the extensive work required. Also, her dad Peter loaned valuable pictures from his service as a Royal Naval Clearance Diver. I am immensely grateful to both of them.'

Only the kind assistance of many people has brought this book to fruition. I would particularly like to place on record the important contribution of Mr Douglas Rendell and Lt Ian 'Shiner' Wrightson RN (the Secretary of the Naval Photographers Association). Additionally, my historical advisers, Paul 'Firestarter' Mayo and Martin 'Jan' Brayley, have been invaluable.

Finally, I am indebted to Mr Alastair Simpson and Mr Peter Coles of Airlife Ltd for the opportunity to produce this book, and for their help throughout my publishing career. The people listed below helped in ways that do not require further elucidation:

Interviews and Manuscript checking: Jan Larcombe, Rod Safe, Ray Bromelow, Francis Saunders, Paul Johnson, John Grant, Doug Rendell, Joe Mendoza, Martin Curtis, Roland Stafford, Joe Caton, Paul Yockney, Pete Holdgate, Brian James, Francis Bulger, Nigel Craft.
Contacts: Mr H. Smith (888 PR Squadron), Mr Alec Rusk (HMS *Hermes* Assn), The Fleet Air Arm Museum, Photographic Department IWM, Mr W.J.G. Spencer PRO, Lt May-Clingo (JSOP), Andy Wing (Stoke Gallery artist).
Contributors: Alastair Campbell, Dave Trish, John 'Fez' Parker, Neil Hall, Eric Kennelly, Chris North, 'Dizzy' de Silva, Kevin Preece, Alan Ferguson, Richie Moss, Steve Saywell, Steve Lewis, Tim Hall, 'Matt' Wellings, Richard Thompson, Richard Glazier (Retired, hurt), and Rex Morgan.

And finally: My friends, who always suffer; 'Wolfie' and Rosie Wilkinson (stars), my career drinking partner 'Iggy' Smith, Stan and Lorraine Bowes, Barney 'live round' Barnes and Maggie, Dave and Mrs Thexton, Dave and Caroline Trish. Peter Russell at the Military Picture Library for good career advice from a gentleman. Eileen Mayo and Julie Russell – chefs par excellence. My oldest friends – my brothers – Keith, Doctor Stuart and Sam the computer man. A big thank you to Fosters Ice Beer/Blue Label Vodka/Mansun/Suede. Medical cover was courtesy of Dr Julian K. Sutton BA, BMBCh, MRCP(UK). Read for defamation by Mr A.R. Jaffa, Foot & Bowden, Exeter.

HMS *Royal Oak* leads the Home Fleet 1936.

FOREWORD

As a proud descendant of Admiral George Anson, one of our nation's most illustrious naval heroes, I am often struck that the accounts of his epic circumnavigation (1740 to 1744) would have been made even more fascinating had they been accompanied by photographs of the events described.

Alas, we had to wait another one hundred years for the invention that has now become commonplace. The Services were quick to make use of this new technology (Crimea and War of Independence - Fenton and Brady) and Shackleton's and Scott's voyages are vivid to us now as a result of the excellence of the photographs that remain as testimony to their tremendous courage and endeavour.

On leaving the regular army to become a professional photographer in the early '60s, the era of national service was coming to an end, and delivered into 'Civvy Street' were thousands of young men who had a grounding in many crafts that would be of lifelong use to them in their chosen careers.

Amongst them were former members of the Royal Naval Photographic Branch which was formed in 1919 and is rightly credited with producing some of the first photographs in the Services.

This book traces the fascinating development from the earliest years to the present, culminating in a colour portfolio of superb work. I am pleased to see such a high level of proficiency exists within the Royal Naval Photographic Branch and sincerely hope that it may long continue to provide such a dynamic record of our Royal Navy.

THE EARL OF LICHFIELD

GENESIS

R atings eligible for, and desirous of joining, the Photographic Branch, should apply to their Commanding Officers'. Thus read paragraph six of Admiralty Fleet Order (AFO) number 3444, issued in November 1919 and appearing between administrative arrangements for 'Submarine Storage Battery Cells – Allowance for Cleaning' and 'Medical Services to Personnel of Merchant Vessels'. Consolidating Admiralty correspondence N10837 of 23 September 1919 and entitled 'Photographic Branch – Non-Substantive Ratings', the order laid out the provisions for placing the fleet's photographic work on a permanent footing. From this inauspicious start grew the Royal Naval photographic specialisation, which developed further into the Branch which still exists today, albeit severely truncated and under significant threat from misguided rationalisation.

The origins of the photographic task within the Royal Navy can be traced back to the requirements of the Grand Fleet in the closing stages of the First World War. Civilian press photographers were employed under the control of the Public Information Officer to the Admiralty, Rear-Admiral Sir Douglas Brownrigg Bt., who also censored every picture that was released to the media. However, the Fleet clearly desired that naval photographic requirements should be met using its own resources, without resort to 'civvies', causing Rear-Admiral Brownrigg to report to the Admiralty;

'The attitude of the Fleet towards (civilian) photographers, both "still" and "moving", was curious. It invariably tried to prevent them being sent up, saying that there were plenty of men in the Fleet capable of doing all that was required. Every artifice and stratagem down to downright lying and misuse of high official's names had to be put in use to succeed in planting my professional photographers and cinematographers in the Fleet on these occasions. I tried hard to explain to them that, however good an amateur may be at ordinary photography, he could not, in the ordinary nature of things, ever expect or hope to be able to compete with the professional'.

It may be persuasively argued that this contemporary evidence of Fleet determination to meet requirements internally would have translated itself into the intention to form a photographic specialisation. Additionally, the arms race that preceded World War One saw the introduction of progressively larger calibre guns, associated complex fire-control and the growth of a doctrine advocating concentration of firepower for effect. Brutally demonstrated at the Battle of Jutland on 31 May 1916, the high degree of gunnery efficiency achieved by the Imperial German Navy indicated to the Admiralty that recording and accuracy of gunnery would have to be placed on the same scientific basis as other rapidly-evolving specialist military disciplines. Accurate gunnery analysis clearly depended on the recording of weapon performance in the environment it was designed for – the Sea.

Analysis of where shells land in relation to the target, known in naval parlance as 'fall of shot', yields valuable data for fine-tuning gun and fire-control systems to ensure maximum accuracy. This analysis was first undertaken using a 'rake' marker, with the centre of the scale centred on the target and the 'prongs' used to indicate degrees of under- or overshoot. Fall of shot was read off at speed where the splashes initially appeared – an essential distinction bearing in mind the size of the column of water produced by a shell the weight of a Mini car – and the distances were called out by the Rake Marking Officer for noting down by a rating. However, with no means of recording the impacts of the shells, this method remained prey to the subjectivity and skill of the observer, particularly as a small lateral displacement of the eye behind the backsight would produce a large error. The introduction of camera recording allowed the measurement of image distance between the target and splash from the negative, simple formulae giving the actual distance. Photography, therefore, was seen as a valuable tool both to enable a permanent record to be made and to objectively increase accuracy.

The Americans had also recognised the value of a permanent record of gunnery data, appearing to have understood the military value of photography very quickly after its applications for aerial reconnaissance had been successfully demonstrated on the Western Front. By 1916, American battleships had begun to use photography for gunnery records and when the 6th Battle Squadron (BATDIV 6) – USS *New York*, USS *Texas*, USS *Wyoming* and USS *Arkansas* – arrived in the UK on 17 December 1917 it brought specialised equipment and personnel for photographic analysis of fall of shot. This equipment proved superior to the conventional method of rake assessment with the naked eye. As a result, some of the equipment was obtained from the Americans and volunteers were sought to form a Fleet Marking Party. The Fleet Marking Party appears to have been at work between the end of the Great War and the issue of the Admiralty Fleet Order detailing formation of the specialisation, as some ratings were able to gain experience in triangulation of fall of shot.

On the cessation of hostilities the Admiralty decided to continue the photographic method of gunnery assessment, a decision no doubt assisted by the Americans, who left some equipment behind on their departure. With this and other surplus material, a 'Royal Navy Photographic Section' was introduced by the Admiralty Fleet Order of 1919, intended as a Seaman branch sub-specialisation open to Seaman ratings and Marines previously employed on fleet photographic tasks. The qualification was additional (non-substantive) and ratings had to combine their own specialisation (torpedoman etc.) with photographic duties, all of which were initially related to gunnery exercises. The additional qualification badge was red and worn on the right cuff, in the same manner as a Ship's Diver, and the extra rate of pay for this task was one shilling per day for a Photographer 1st Class. Rating volunteers had to be recommended by Commanding Officers as competent photographers, with particulars of their experience forwarded with applications to the Admiralty. Six ratings were originally required, but eleven ratings volunteered and were accepted.

The man tasked with the formation of the specialisation was a Paymaster Lieutenant in the Royal Naval Reserve, who had previously served in this capacity on the staff of Admiral Sir Charles E. Madden GCB KCMG CVO – Commander-in-Chief of the Atlantic Fleet. In October 1919 Lieutenant Humphrey Joel RNR was appointed the first Fleet Photographic Officer in the Royal Navy, responsible to the Admiral and remaining on his staff, borne in HMS *Queen Elizabeth*. Lieutenant Joel clearly had a significant interest in photography, a fact that almost certainly led to his appointment, and his technical competence is indicated by his later employment as the photographer to the Bank of England and Lloyds of London. In November 1920 he moved to HMS *Excellent*, again as Photographic Officer; the available evidence suggests that he spent this time laying the foundations of the specialisation. Mr Albert W. Smith was promoted to be the first Commissioned Officer in charge of the Royal Naval School of Photography (RNSOP) on 16 April 1920. The school itself opened at Tipner Ranges in the same year, functioning under the command of HMS *Excellent* – the Royal Navy's Gunnery School located on Whale Island in Portsmouth. The RNSOP is believed to have been one of the oldest dedicated photographic schools in the world.

The first eleven volunteers were given very basic instruction, to a syllabus designed to enable them to undertake naval photography and cinematography. On completion, the first deployment of RN photographers with a common qualification took place when five 2nd class ratings were drafted to sea, while the remaining six photographic ratings remained at the school, establishing darkroom and workrooms. These five ratings joined the 'Arabis' class sloop, HMS *Snapdragon*, which was serving as the target-towing ship for the Atlantic Fleet, tasked to accompany HM Ships *Queen Elizabeth* (flagship), *Barham*, *Royal Sovereign*, *Ramilles* and *Royal Oak* on the spring cruise of 1920. Sailing on Friday 16 January, the ratings were further instructed in triangulation, plotting of fall of shot and gained practical experience of stand/hand cameras and 35mm cine cameras. The fleet visited Gibraltar, Palma, Algiers and Malta on this deployment, taking the opportunity to practise weaponry as opportunity presented itself. The Report of Proceedings for this cruise, submitted to the Admiralty on return of the flagship, mentions 'Full Calibre Firings' of 15-inch main armament on 26 February and 15 March 1920. These exercises are the first recorded time that the new Branch was utilised at sea. As Lieutenant Joel was recorded as the Fleet Photographic Officer on the flagship, there can be little doubt that this initial trial was personally supervised by him. Returning to Plymouth on 27 March from this deployment, these ratings then exchanged with the six other photographers at Tipner. Additionally, around this time a small amount of routine internal photographic work started to flow from Portsmouth Dockyard, demanding the wider technical application of still camera work.

In March 1921, a further Admiralty Fleet Order announced the examination for Photographer 1st Class, the syllabus having already been promulgated by the same method. This examination syllabus provides an illuminating glimpse into the fledgling Branch, requiring immediate successful completion for confirmation in existing rates and establishing joining criteria that have echoed down the years. The examination itself was in three parts, written, practical and cinema work, showing the surprisingly detailed knowledge deemed necessary for naval photographic applications at that time:

Admiralty Fleet Order 3444 of November 1919, which started the Royal Naval Photographic Branch. (Reproduced by permission of the Public Records Office, Kew.)

53   **3440**

3440.—Submarine Storage Battery Cells—Allowance for Cleaning, &c.

(C. Sec. P.L. 735/19.—18.10.1919.)

The instructions issued in M.O. 735/19, relative to the allowances to be paid to workpeople when engaged in cleaning and refilling storage cells with acid in connection with the repair of Submarine batteries, are extended to cover similar employment in connection with other storage batteries where the conditions in respect of which the allowances are payable are comparable to those obtaining in the case of Submarine storage batteries.

(*M.O. 735/19.*)

3444.—Photographic Branch—Non-Substantive Ratings.

(N. 10837.—23.9.1919.)

With a view to placing the photographic work of the Fleet on a permanent footing, it has been decided to institute the non-substantive ratings of Photographer, 1st Class, and Photographer, 2nd Class, for which ratings of the Seaman Branch and Marines will be eligible.

2. Candidates for the Photographic Branch must have previous experience in photography, and must hold no other higher non-substantive rating than Gunlayer, 2nd Class, at the date of application. They must be recommended by their Commanding Officers as competent Photographers, and particulars must be given of their previous photographic experience, especially in Fleet work, such as triangulation of fall of shot.

3. The non-substantive pay attached to the new Branch will be:—

	s.	d.
Photographer, 1st Class – – – – – –	1	0 per diem.
Photographer, 2nd Class – – – – – –	0	6 ,, ,,

4. Ratings previously employed on Fleet Photographic work, and recommended for the new Branch, who are not Seamen or Marines, may, if selected, be allowed to transfer to the rank of Private, R.M.L.I.

5. The number of Photographers who will be selected immediately is six. These will be drafted to H.M.S. "Snapdragon" for service with the Atlantic Fleet. The requirements of Photographic Personnel in future, at home and abroad, are, however, under consideration, and further orders will be issued when these are decided, together with regulations governing the qualifications for 1st and 2nd Class rates.

6. Ratings eligible for, and desirous of joining, the Photographic Branch should apply to their Commanding Officers, who will forward their applications through the usual channels with particulars as laid down in paragraph 2.

7. Recommendations should reach the Admiralty at the earliest possible date and for the present are limited to ratings serving in Home Waters and the Mediterranean.

(*C.I.O. 1256/19 is cancelled.*)

3445.—Medical Services to Personnel of Merchant Vessels.

(N.L. 29694.—1.11.1919.)

A case has recently occurred in which a financial claim has been made by a Naval Medical Officer for services rendered, in respect of an urgently necessary operation performed in an emergency in one of H.M. Ships upon a member of the crew of a merchant vessel. The Admiralty consider it to be one of the duties of H.M. Navy to assist merchant shipping in distress and to afford medical attendance to the personnel in urgent cases without consideration of financial reward.

Action of this kind, however, requiring operative or other serious treatment at the hands of a Naval Medical Officer should be limited to actual cases of emergency, and in such cases no charge should be made, except to the extent of the actual expenditure of stores, payment for which should be credited to the public funds.

Written	Use of panchromatic plates and filters Detailed knowledge of photographic chemicals and defects met in photography Elementary knowledge of photographic lenses, such as names and uses, including the telephoto lens Names of principal aberrations and defects which may be expected in a lens Definition of terms used in connection with lenses Calculation of conjugate foci
Practical	Ability to use a focal-plane or reflex camera effectively Intensifying or reducing a negative Enlarging Lantern slide making by reduction or contact

Dry and wet mounting
Knowledge of flashlight photography and precautions necessary
Blocking out and spotting a negative
Loading up and developing plates in darkness
Taking charge of a developing party working triangulation film
To be able to plot fall of shot from the triangulation camera prints

Cinema work   Loading and operating a cinema camera
Developing and printing a film

Five of the original ratings sat the exam in March 1921, of which three passed, including acting Photographer 2nd Class Percy Forrow. When the need for a further formal instructional syllabus became apparent, Lieutenant Joel sent for Percy Forrow, informed him of the Admiralty's decision and invited him to become the Royal Navy's first photographic instructor. Promoted immediately to Petty Officer Photographer 1st Class, Percy Forrow accepted and spent over two months assembling diagrams and the instructional programme, having only the examination syllabus at this stage to be his guide. His syllabus of instruction was used virtually unchanged until the Second World War, indicating that PO(Phot) Forrow left an indelible quality hallmark for the Branch.

After approval of his instructional syllabus, PO(Phot) Forrow began to instruct both 1st and 2nd class photographer basic classes and specialised course for officers being appointed as Photographic Officers. In January 1923 Lt-Cdr (G) Quintin B. Preston-Thomas RN was appointed the first Commanding Officer of the RNSOP, the same year that HMS *Chrysanthemum* took over gunnery marking for the Mediterranean Fleet after her conversion for photographic work during the autumn of 1919 in Plymouth. Photographers continued to be supplied to the Atlantic, Mediterranean and China Fleet from Tipner throughout this period for gunnery purposes. Around six ratings were trained per year at the RNSOP, deemed sufficient for maintaining personnel levels to meet the gunnery requirement. CPO(Phot) Forrow was pensioned at the end of his engagement in 1933, being immediately and sensibly retained in the same position as a civilian instructor.

Evidence of the work undertaken by the Branch between the wars is sketchy, but a small amount of information remains in the Public Records Office and related publications. A series of gunnery trials on 20 January 1925 showed the typical employment of photographers at the time. The old battleship HMS *Monarch* was stripped of her armament and towed out to a point south-west of Ireland, where HMS *Snapdragon* waited with elements of the Atlantic Fleet. During the course of the day, the battleships HMS *Revenge, Ramilles, Royal Oak, Resolution* and *Royal Sovereign* of the Seventh Flotilla engaged the target, taking part in 'five-ship concentration trials' and achieving an average shell 'spread' of 700 yards despite laying errors due to target smoke. Following each shoot, destroyers escorted HMS *Snapdragon* close round HMS *Monarch* while photographs of the damage were taken.

Below:
Seen from the stern of a target-towing tug, the recording of 'fall of shot' is the reason the Photographic Branch came into existence. Today, it is difficult to appreciate the sheer violence of war at sea in the early to mid-twentieth century, when giant shells full of high explosive could be fired at targets up to fifteen miles away with great accuracy.

Night engagements followed, in which photography was conducted by searchlight and starshell until the target ship sank just before dawn.

A further insight can be gained from the employment of photographers carried in HMS *Glorious* during 1931. On board, an RAF Corporal Photographer was in charge of the section of two naval ratings and tasking included the filming of each deck landing and gunnery spotting from Nimrod and Fairey 111F aircraft. Visiting VIPs arriving by air were presented with a picture of their arrival as the aircraft was arrested on deck by the Seamen Aircraft Handlers.

Interestingly, Air Photography courses were run by the RAF at Farnborough for aircrew, evidence of a growing awareness of the importance of the medium. Air Publication 1354 (1929) was the reference book for the air photographic task at the time and contains instructions to squadron photographers that have hardly changed over sixty-five years:

> 'arrangements should be made for a photographer from the section to be available whenever an aircraft which has been carrying out air photography returns. As soon as possible after the aircraft has landed he should take charge of the exposed magazines and return them to the photographic section'.

Chapter 6 of the same publication defines the role played by photography:

> 'In time of peace, air photography is used extensively by the Navy in connection with gunnery and torpedo training, photographs of the fall of shot around a target, and of the tracks of torpedoes, being of considerable value to those responsible for directing such operations'.

Below:

Ron 'Tiny' Little joined the Royal Navy on 24 June 1929, serving as an Ordinary Seaman (Gunner), working the photographic sub-specialisation as required. Passing for Photographer 2nd Class in 1935, he was promoted to Acting Leading Photographer in 1937 as part of the Admiralty's policy of promoting those with experience to form the backbone of a new branch. Progressing rapidly through the rates, he achieved promotion to Warrant Rank in 1942 and was commissioned post-war, when he assumed a senior role in the Branch. His pre-war S1246Q Photographer Rating's History Sheet shows that no records were kept under the old system to document the requirements of the profession during this period.

S.—1246Q. (Established—December, 1937.)

PHOTOGRAPHER RATING'S HISTORY SHEET.

To be kept attached to the Rating's Service Certificate and handed to him with it on final discharge from the Service.

Full Name LITTLE Ronald Joseph (Surname in BLOCK LETTERS)   Port Division PORTSMOUTH.   Official No. JX 132406.   MX 56305

EXAMINATION RECORD.
To be filled in according to the result obtained after examination.

Date	Nature of Examination		Still Photography																	Cinema				Sound Recording				Total		Passed or Failed	Initials of Examining Officer

(Column headers: Triangulation, Wet and Dry Mounting, Spotting, Blocking Out and Retouching, Lantern Slide Making, Intensifying and Reducing, Printing and Enlarging, Copying, Flashlight, Stand Cameras (Interior), Hand Cameras, Exposure Calculation, Theory of Photography, Light and Optics, School, Cutting and Editing, Film Processing, Cinema Printing and Titling, Camera Manipulation, Theory, Practice, Theory, Amplifiers, Projection)

Date	Nature of Examination		
1st Oct 1935	For Photographer Part I.	% Required	65 65 65 60 75 60 70 60 60 / 60 50 65 60 / 65 / 60 50 50 65 50 / 60 65 — To Pass 60%
		% Obtained	Old System (No record) — Passed FC
4th April 1938	For Petty Officer Photographer	% Required	80 70 70 70 80 70 80 80 70 70 75 70 80 75 / 70 75 75 80 75 / 65 65 65 80 60 — 70%
		% Obtained	80 89 95 78 93 72 96 90 74 81 100 85 100 88 96 / 85 80 91 95 82 / 74 63 72 100 86⅘ Passed FC approved

	Photographer Part II. (Sea Training)	Recommendation	Ship	Photographic Officer's Initials	Captain's Initials
2/3.39		To be confirmed	Guardian		for Captain

N. 7437/37.   32695/8750 250/3/38 Wt & Sons Ltd 2130*/49519/672   S.—1246Q.

To cast some light on the equipment used at this time, we are fortunate to have the observations of Lt-Cdr Ron 'Tiny' Little RN, an 'old school' photographer who rose from being a junior rating on the 'lower deck' in the early days of the Branch to assume a pivotal role in post-war policy as an officer. Pre-war cameras and equipment in use with the specialisation included many types that are now extremely valuable and rare. Thornton Pickard half plate and quarter plate hand cameras gave a focal plane shutter speed of up to 1/1000 of a second, opening up to a maximum f4.5 and therefore used for hand-held applications. Larger Sanderson stand cameras fulfilled the technical and copy role, with a selection of specialist Mk 3 and Mk 4 Dial Recording Cameras used for documenting the settings on gunnery fire-control systems.

The 'miniature' cameras available were the Leica Mk 1 and Mk 3, fitted with 2-inch lenses opening up to f1.9. Exposure normally depended on the skill of the photographer, as the Watkins Bee light meters were rare. The stock comment on exposure if asked for advice was, 'Give it 1/100 at f8 and stop down a bit'. Developers such as MQ, Metol, Amidol and caustic hydroquinone were mixed from raw chemicals, a time-consuming and hazardous job which left some doubt if any two mixes were ever the same. Mixes were, unsurprisingly, used to exhaustion, processing the Ilford Double Express ortho plates and Special Rapid Panchromatic available. Flash photography could also be undertaken using 'open shutter' methods, but was a highly dangerous business as the Sashalite flashbulbs used could explode or sympathetically ignite all the other bulbs in the area. Special Low Angle Marking cameras were developed for the recording of gunnery, capable of making one exposure every second, or two every three seconds. They were fitted with a stopwatch and a disc on which all the relevant data about the shoot could be recorded, illuminated by auxiliary lighting from a battery and photographed onto the film. Considerable proficiency was required to sight the splashes, train the camera, start the watch and make the exposure in the limited time available.

By 1935 there were about fifty ratings in the Branch and ships were beginning to be designed with specially prepared photographic facilities – the net layers *Guardian* and *Protector* were the first ships to incorporate darkroom compartments. High speed battle practice targets were also introduced to the fleet at this time, bringing a more realistic training device into service for gunnery firings. Fleet photographic personnel transferred as required to the light cruisers towing these targets, notably 'Arethusa' class light cruisers. A typical employment of photographic ratings was recording the 40-salvo prolonged test firing of HMS *Warspite*'s heavy guns in May 1938, carried out to prove the new 30-degree mountings and fire-control system. Mr Bill Barber, later a civilian instructor at RNSOP but a photographic rating at this time, had graphic memories of HMS *Barham*'s big guns during the assessment of accuracy by another means – the 'throw-off' method first developed in 1917. In this type of practice, the fire-control systems of the firing ship were aimed at the target ship, with the guns system adjusted (or 'thrown-off') by a known angle (normally five degrees) to ensure that the shells landed aft. Mr Barber recalled that the *Barham*'s gunners were not always completely accurate when setting degrees of 'throw off', resulting in considerable danger to the analysis party. The hazardous nature of these gunnery shoots can only be imagined. Despite the non-substantive nature of the early photographic specialisation at this time, contemporary records indicate that excellent results were obtained, used by the fleet for analysis and forwarded with records as an insurance against cheating.

SECOND WORLD WAR

After many representations, and as the storm clouds of war approached, the Admiralty finally recognised the clear need for new and larger specialisation, mainly to meet the urgent requirements of the rapidly expanding Fleet Air Arm. On 18 June 1937 an Order in Council published in the *London Gazette* announced that sanction had been given for a substantive Photographic Branch.

ROYAL NAVAL SCHOOL OF PHOTOGRAPHY

New Eyes Of The Fleet

THE NAVY is to have its own photographers and cine-camera men.

A school has been opened in H.M.S. Excellent (Whale Island, Portsmouth), where all

Left:
After the initial period of ill-preparation, Britain's rearming for the inevitable war ahead was jingoistically reported in the newspapers and periodicals of the time. Here, the *Illustrated London News* announces the formation of the Phot School in 1938.

The Navy magazine of April 1938 featured an article called 'The Camera and the Fleet', which announced in the typically surreal idiolect of the times:

'The modern Navy is increasingly what may be called abreast of the times, and this tendency is exemplified in the formation of a photographic training school at Whale Island. This gunning with a camera, which has long been the hobby of big game hunters in their hours of ease, is something quite new for HMS *Excellent* but not the less likely to serve and increase the complete efficiency of the Royal Navy. Certainly the Whale Island School presents boys with a new opportunity of combining a particular hobby with a general sea service.'

On 24 June 1937, Admiralty Fleet Order 1279/37 instituted and announced the formation of this new Branch of the Royal Navy, consolidated by the comprehensive AFO 'Photographer Ratings – Institution of Substantive Branch' that followed in January 1938. Entry requirements, vision and educational standards were all laid down, together with details of status ('Photographic ratings are classed as "daymen" and do not exercise military command') and dress. The number of ratings needed was recognised to be considerably in excess of that previously required, and a minimum target of twenty-four men to be trained per year was ordered. Volunteers

Right:
After the new Branch had been established by Admiralty Fleet Order 1279/37, it was recognised that cine and associated sound recording would be a necessary skill for the future. The sound recording set-up seen here is believed to be the first that the Branch possessed and is being tested outside the newly constructed Film Studio at Tipner. 'Tiny' Little is seated second from the left.

Above:
A month of basic theoretical instruction took place at HMS *Excellent*, designed to reject unsuitable candidates before they progressed to the RNSOP. A group of suitably diligent ratings watch intently as the Petty Officer instructor teaches the basics of optical theory in 1938.

were again requested to submit documents and conduct sheets to the Captain of HMS *Excellent*, who remained the controlling authority for the Branch, allocating course places as they became available. Ratings from the previous non-substantive photographic specialistion were subsumed into the new Branch at a higher level, given exemption from basic instruction, and formed the experienced backbone of the new Branch. Photographic Rating's History Sheets (S–1246Q) were commenced at this time, and it is interesting to note that the existing ratings who 'transferred' to the new Branch had no records under the old system.

As part of this process, CPO Frank Ebling (8 June 1937) and CPO George Crouch (3 April 1939) were promoted to be the first Warrant Photographers to oversee the school. Additionally, in recognition of the increasingly important role of film-making, the Film Studio at Tipner was constructed in 1937 and rudimentary film sound recording for the production of instructional films began. Williamson and Vinten 35mm cine cameras were introduced to the fledging cine side, which developed film secured to pin frames holding 200ft of film, processed in 20 gallon teak tanks. The RNSOP had the only processing machine in the fleet, constant monitoring of which was needed to catch any break in the film.

The first month of photographic training for prospective photographic ratings took place at HMS *Excellent* and was designed to weed out unsuitable candidates. It consisted of maths, chemistry, light and optics, after which the trainee had a further fifteen weeks at the RNSOP Tipner. This instructional phase introduced the mixing of developers, fixers, reducers and intensifiers, camera equipment being introduced after a month. A heavy Soho Ruby reflex half plate camera remained indelibly imprinted on some minds, as when the mirror went up to make the exposure it nearly knocked the photographer out! This phase was followed by a three-month sea-going placement in a target vessel, which indicates the importance still placed on gunnery recording. A trainee at the time, Photo(A) Gordon Herd, remembers 'Fall of shot recording, which was apparently developed in Edwardian times. It involved the use of fearsome-looking cameras that resembled pieces of artillery and took negatives of immense proportions'. Photographic ratings messed at HMS *Excellent* throughout, marching to and from Tipner via the foreshore twice a day – eight miles in all, plus a further distance some nights to 'The Beresford' public house in Rudmore. Instruction took place in a large wooden hut which was divided roughly into four – a classroom at each end with two darkrooms in the middle, all joined by light traps. The darkrooms had large sinks in the middle of the room and could be used from all sides. There was also a store, chemical mixing room and instructor's office. Two classes progressed through the school three months apart, with 15–20

trainees on each, and by early 1939 the 5th Photographers' Qualifying Course (QC) was undergoing instruction at Tipner.

The 5th QC was the first course to be sent to RAF Ford instead of the sea-going course element on completion, the purpose of which was to learn aerial photographic techniques, taught by Royal Air Force instructors. This change marked the beginning of a new emphasis on the air side of photography and in recognition of the Fleet Air Arm's pre-eminent requirement for photography, the Branch was transferred from the control of the Gunnery Division to Director of Airfields and Carrier Requirements (DACR) in late 1939.

Photographic ratings were intended to be distributed when numbers permitted as detailed below:

To each private capital ship, cruiser and flotilla leader	1 Leading Photographer
To each capital ship and cruiser flagship	2 Photographers
To each netlayer employed in the Fleet Target Service	1 CPO Photographer 1 PO Photographer 1 Leading Photographer 3 Photographers
To each flagship (where no Photographic Officer is borne)	1 PO Photographer (if triangulation equipment is supplied) 1 Leading Photographer
To RN Photographic School	1 Warrant Photographer 2 CPO Photographers 3 PO Photographers 7 Leading Photographers, plus drafting margin for courses

Deployed photographers were further allocated into the fleet as follows:

Home Fleet	–	OIC+5 ratings
Atlantic Fleet	–	OIC+5 ratings
Mediterranean Fleet	–	OIC+5 ratings
China Fleet	–	2 ratings

The advent of the Second World War saw the Fleet Air Arm in considerable disarray; equipped with obsolete aircraft, administration only recently wrested from the RAF and a huge operational task. Responsibility for photographic services and support had only been handed over in the year war broke out.

AN INSTRUCTOR SAYS WHAT IS WANTED: *"This is the Angle from which you Shoot."*
There are naval photographers out over the North Sea and the coast of Norway. On aerodromes and aircraft-carriers others stand by ready to take
over. Still more are in training. They are the eyes of the Navy, and of the Navy's bombers.

anything of note, they were to record it photo- | R.A.F. machines. They were sailors, however, as | At a level 3,000 feet they covered the first
graphically for his benefit. | well as airmen, the weather was good, and they | eighty miles and from that height saw the steep
Not for them the cabined comfort of present day | were used to flying in their open-cockpit plane. | Norwegian coast rise before them. Then, to

The Apparatus is Prepared . . . | *Loading for the Flight* . . . | *The Film is Developed at Speed* . . .
It is an automatic aerial camera. It | *A sailor hands up the loaded camera* | *As the plane lands, the films are handed over the side and rushed*
has had many triumphs already in | *to the naval photographer in the plane.* | *. . . to the developing room.*
the war.

The Royal Air Force made the first of many significant contributions to the
Branch at this initial stage, instructing trainees, providing equipment and in
many cases actually supplying personnel to manage sections on ships until
sufficient naval Petty Officers became available in late 1940. The issue of
using RAF cameras and darkroom equipment began at this time. It was
considerably better than none at all but limited in application, as the RAF was
primarily concerned with airborne needs which did not allow the flexibility
required by the RN. The RAF Manual of Photography (AP 1354) was used
as the Book of Reference (BR) throughout the War.

At the outbreak of the Second World War, photographic ratings were being
trained to undertake the following tasks:

- Photographic plotting of surface shoots for line/rake
- Line marking of AA practices
- Iron printing processes
- Stand and press photography
- Technical photograph reproduction
- Air photography
- Cinemaphotography including projection
- Sound recording – to a limited extent
- Various types of finishing processes

Training was also unable to keep pace with the wider requirements of
wartime photography, therefore the Branch was further sub-divided into

three smaller specialisations – the RN Film Unit, Cinema Operators (Cameramen) and Admiralty Press Photographers.

In late 1940, the first Hostilities Only (HO) ratings photographic course commenced, and by spring 1941 the 14th course was underway, illustrating the high throughput of students at the time. Many of these conscripted trainees commented unfavourably on the wider aspects of naval service, including Commander's Rounds at HMS *Excellent* and the necessarily large number of trainees, all of which seemed to militate against actually achieving any competence in the photographic trade. The trainees, and indeed the Branch at this time, also had to contend with the label 'a bunch of bloody queers', advanced by some of the more intellectually challenged specialists at the finest Gunnery School in the world, Whale Island. This label reflects the animosity and level of prejudice generally felt by the members of the Gunnery Branch at this time, photographic staff often being the cause of bad news after 'successful' shoots and also perceived as outsiders to the General Service.

The course now consisted of three months' naval instruction at Tipner, where Service instructors, normally regulars from pre-war days, were assisted by the redoubtable Barber brothers, William (Bill) and Jack, now attached to the school as civilians after their naval experiences. The brothers were clearly staunch supporters of naval photography and a classic quotation from William Barber may be found in the *Practical Photographer* magazine (February, 1961), when he was still instructing at the RNSOP:

Above:
Portsmouth and the concentration of military activity in the area were clearly significant targets for the German *Luftwaffe*, who employed accurate photo-analysis in planning air raids. This picture, taken at 1410 hours on 18 September 1940 by *Oblt* Junghans from a reconnaissance aircraft, shows the aftermath of an attack on 'Hafenanlage Portsmouth', complete with annotation of various targets for future action. In particular, Portsmouth Harbour station, projecting into the harbour, can be seen burning, as well as the location of several RN capital ships. It is reasonable to assume that these pictures were used to plan further attacks, as Portsmouth suffered its own 'blitz' shortly afterwards. The location of the RNSOP is ringed. (*Luftwaffe* via Peter Russell).

Above:
In addition to receiving instruction, ratings were required to keep security duties at the school and firewatching duties elsewhere in Portsmouth. This classic period shot shows Photo(A) Arthur 'Barney' Barnes on security duty outside the building now used as Boss 1's office, with the entrance to the site behind him. 'Barney' volunteered for the Branch in 1939, successfully completing training in 1941. After a short spell as staff at Tipner, he was drafted to HMS *Nile* in Alexandria, providing phot services to the fleet including low angle gunnery marking. The black dog seen here, belonging to the Commander, was nicknamed 'Hypo' and was well known to the trainees. The two low buildings on the left survive, used as the crewroom for today's RN photographers. Guard duty at the time was undertaken with a rifle but no ammunition to hand – the five rounds available were held by the Officer of the Day.

Right:
Naval photographers have been and still are afforded unpredented access to the men and material of the fleet. This public relations picture, taken by an unknown naval photographer, captures the youth of the crew and the might of the battleship HMS *Hood*, which was soon destined to die with only three survivors. It is a great sadness that the names of the ratings do not survive, only that of the dog – 'Bill'.

'I joined the service in 1915, I became a photographer in 1932. In 1938 I stayed in the service as a civilian photographer, and I am still going strong – it can't be too bad, can it?'

Six weeks billeted at Felpham, Bognor Regis, followed for the basic trainees whilst they received air instruction in F24 cameras, printing, mosaic making and overlaps at RAF Ford. A high premium was placed on the ability to use and repair the F24, an abiding memory of many being the requirement to learn the complete mechanical cycle of operations of this superb camera. Hand-held and fixed camera techniques were taught, along with subsequent use of darkroom equipment for processing and printing. Following a long tradition, the local church at Climping was used to practise architectural interiors and exteriors. The opportunity was taken wherever possible to give photographers air experience, either in the obsolete Blackburn Sharks at the station or the Avro Anson communication aircraft. The training involved vertical overlap practice and inevitable aerial photographs of Arundel Castle at the end of the sortie. On completion of the course, photographers were rated and sent to the fleet as required, normally on the day after completion.

By late 1940 the training programme had produced enough photographers to start filling billets in the fleet and ships began to receive their complements. Two ratings were supplied to each capital ship and one to each squadron, bringing the number of ratings typically to four on an aircraft carrier. The primary role of ratings became common to the fleet over time and included bridge duties at action/harbour stations, coverage of flight deck incidents, battle damage recording and basic public relations photography. Squadron ratings were responsible for the loading of camera magazines, processing of reconnaissance and also joined in as required in a ship's tasking.

RABBITS

Around this time another function of the Branch was legitimised by RN Regulations, subsequently becoming a tradition that cast a long and murky shadow until the early 1990s. Intended by the Admiralty to encourage further use of equipment to achieve higher proficiency, the sale of pictures to naval personnel for private retention also had a secondary 'public relations' motive (the theory being that ratings would purchase these pictures, take them home and show them around, thus assisting recruitment). The sale and production of these pictures became known colloquially within the Royal Navy and the Branch as 'rabbit' work. This unusual term has its origins in the 1860s, when the expansion of Chatham dockyard necessitated the purchase of land riddled with rabbits. These rabbits therefore belonged to the MoD and were stolen despite severe penalties for offenders. Over time, in a naval context the word came to mean 'presents', particularly those made on board using materials from Service sources. Now a generic term implying any connection with these activities, the business operated by a section was (and still is) collectively known as a 'rabbit' firm, started after the time-honoured naval procedure of submitting a request form to the Commander.

Left:
Evidence of the humour that 'rabbits' or private work has caused in the Branch over the years can be seen in this contemporary drawing, produced by Photo(A) Ford for the Gibraltar photographic section, Christmas 1944. Note that after serving on an aircraft carrier, the rabbit goes straight to the bank.

Unfortunately, private recompense immediately became a significant bonus of becoming a Navy photographer. Contemporary accounts indicate that small fortunes were made by selling prints even at this relatively early juncture, with prices fixed by the Commander of the respective ship or unit. While 'private' film, paper and chemicals for 'firms' were supposed to be purchased ashore, the relaxed attitude of many ratings towards this material was public and that which 'belonged to the firm' created a system open to abuse. This anomaly has only been effectively closed in the recent past and accounts for the large fortunes amassed by many naval photographers throughout the years until the mid-1990s.

The scope for private enterprise can be imagined from a large Ship's Company photograph alone; even in 1944, when the battleship HMS *King George V* had a group picture taken by ratings from HMS *Dunluce Castle* in Scapa Flow, the resulting print sold over one thousand copies at one shilling and six pence a time. It should, however, be borne in mind that this was a service provided out of normal hours of ratings employment and was also enthusiastically welcomed by the servicemen 'customers'.

This permission has also successfully motivated Navy photographers to this

Above:
Taken on a whole plate camera by two RN photographers of the Fleet Requirements Unit, based on board the depot ship HMS *Dunluce Castle*, this Ship's Company group of HMS *King George V* sold a vast amount of copies at one shilling and sixpence (7½p in today's money). Douglas Rendell comments, 'With over 1500 men on board and little to spend their money on, there was a big demand for prints and it was almost impossible not to become involved.

day, as a good shot on an aircraft carrier will still sell hundreds of copies. It would be imprudent to reveal figures attained by some 'rabbit' firms on ships today; suffice to say that the amounts have successfully kept up with inflation. Generally, Ship's Captains were keen on the sale of prints to the Ship's Company, some ratings even being ordered to operate them, as ten per cent of the profits was always donated to the Ship's Welfare Fund. The term 'rabbit' has contributed greatly to Branch humour over the years, not least in the labelling of one rating on board an aircraft carrier in the 1950s as 'myxomatosis', because he always 'f**ked up the rabbits'.

Right:
Routine record photography from the War today shows us the fascinating reality of a global conflict in a past information age, when a letter missed by the censor really could cause a security breach. Five hundred letters per day were written by the Ship's Company, which must have proved less than fascinating reading for the unfortunate officers during their tea breaks.

ACTION

As we follow the progression of the Second World War, it is difficult to generalise about the careers of photographers once they had left the school, because the vagaries of the naval drafting system and the size of the organisation meant that some never went to sea, some never flew and some never even met another photographer. Some never saw the enemy, while others came into regular contact through the vicious war being fought at sea. Regulations for photographers at sea included the fateful statement, 'During Action Stations a Photographer's Duty is on the bridge to photograph any action that may arise'. This order led to some astonishing acts of bravery.

Photo(A) John Grant joined the RN as a boy seaman and was serving on board HMS *Revenge* when he volunteered for the Photographic Branch after the 1937 AFO was pinned up on noticeboards through the fleet. At Tipner the day that war was declared, as soon as his course finished he was drafted to HMS *Glorious*. Travelling out to meet the ship in the Mediterranean, he and Photo(A) 'Master' Furlong missed the carrier several times and had to return home, by which time the Commander at Tipner had decided to send someone else. They were therefore not aboard on the fateful day of 8 June 1940, when the ship was annihilated by the German pocket battleships *Scharnhorst* and *Gneiseneau* off Norway, killing the entire photographic section. Photo(A) 'Buck' Taylor's body was recovered, but his two shipmates were not so fortunate. Photo(A) B. 'Nobby' Clarke, who had met his wife locally on the morning march to Tipner for instruction, was lost in the action and is today commemorated on panel 42 of the imposing Plymouth Royal Naval Memorial, whilst his workmate, Photo(A) John Moody, is recorded on panel 43 of the Portsmouth Memorial, after being killed in the same terrible slaughter.

Mercifully, the loss of life amongst the specialisation was generally very low, although over a dozen RN photographers lost their lives during the War. This includes the ratings on HMS *Repulse* and HMS *Prince of Wales* when they were sunk by the Japanese, plus the sections on board HMS *Dasher* (petrol explosion off Scotland) and HMS *Avenger* (torpedoed in 1942). Photo(A) Hurley and another rating died on the flight deck of HMS *Hermes* in the same year whilst doing their duty under attack from the Japanese. Additionally, Leading Photo(A) F. Chuter is recorded on panel 79 of the Portsmouth Memorial under the year 1943, killed in a flying accident, as were two ratings from the Fleet Requirements Unit detailed later in the text. During the overnight Battle of Narvik 27/28 May 1940, Photo(A) Newstead was wounded by German fire, evacuated safely during the withdrawal and awarded a gallantry medal. The section on HMS *Courageous* was more fortunate when the ship was torpedoed south-west of Ireland by U-29 on 17 September 1939. In age-old cavalier photographic rating style, the men were playing an illegal gambling game of pontoon, door locked, when the carrier was struck by a torpedo. The impact knocked the key out of the door as the lights went out, so the first task was to scrabble about the floor in pitch darkness to find the key before escaping.

Photo(A) Grant then joined HMS *Illustrious*, which launched the devastating raid on the Italian Fleet at Taranto on 11 November 1940. This attack was driven by naval interpretation of RAF reconnaissance, from inception to post-raid analysis. The photographic section played an important part in processing all the raid pictures taken by the observers with hand-held cameras. The section also played a key role in the planning of the attack itself, because the only set of accurate reconnaissance pictures was 'borrowed' from

Below:
Douglas Rendell progressed from Photo(A) to Sub-Lieutenant during the War, serving on board HMS *King George V* for the visit of the King in 1943. The darkroom on board was minuscule, nine feet square which just allowed the full extension of a camp bed and was situated on the main deck amidships. Apart from some processing tanks and dishes, equipment consisted solely of a Van Neck Press camera and a half plate autofocus enlarger. In traditional style, the enlarger shivered and shook when the ship was at speed, as the movement was transmitted through the bulkhead to the enlarger head. This phenomenon continues to this day on RN ships. The mark of the true seagoing naval photographer remains that of having looked through the magnifier whilst printing at sea and observed the vibrating silver halide grain of the projected image on the baseboard. Even to this day, naval photographers in darkrooms repeat the traditional lines 'Ours is not to reason why, ours is just to print and dry'.

the RAF analysis cell in Cairo by the ship's Photographic Interpreter Lt David Pollock RNVR, copied on board and replaced before detection. The success of this audacious raid by Fleet Air Arm Swordfish on Taranto so antagonised Mussolini that he personally approached Hitler, requesting the loan of two crack dive-bombing squadrons in order to sink the *Illustrious*. The Junkers Ju 87 (*Stuka*) units finally caught up with the ship on 10 January 1941, whilst she was escorting a convoy on Operation *Excess*. Shortly after midday, the ship closed up to action stations, with Photo(A) Grant on the bridge with his F24 camera fitted with a 5-inch lens. For the next eight hours the *Illustrious* was attacked and severely damaged, taking six direct hits including one that blew the after hangar lift and aircraft over the side. Throughout this time Photo(A)s Grant and Furlong stayed on the bridge, taking some astonishing action pictures which depicted the *Stukas* forming up, attacking in the dive, and the dreadful carnage below on the flight deck and gun positions.

At nightfall the ship was towed into Malta, where for the next five days she was attacked alongside in Valletta Harbour, such was the determination to sink her. Once again the phot team was in action, taking pictures of the dockyard under attack and documenting the dreadful damage on board. HMS *Illustrious* was so badly damaged that she had to go to the United States for repair. Grant was left behind to augment the phots in Malta.

Photo(A) Grant finally managed to gain passage to Gibraltar in November 1941, but was amazed on reporting to the docks to discover he was taking passage on HM Submarine *Regent*. The journey to Gibraltar took twelve days, surfacing at night and running deep during the day. This unusual journey became even more so when the *Regent* engaged and sunk a supply ship with gunfire – he was co-opted to pass up the ammunition. HM submarine *Regent* was subsequently lost, sunk with all hands in the Gulf of Taranto after striking an enemy mine on 16 April 1943.

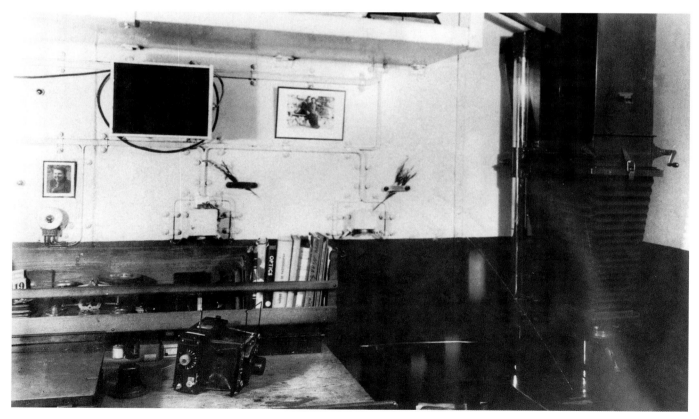

Photographers in other theatres of war at sea had different experiences. Photo(A) Douglas Rendell noted with wry amusement the vibration and shock imparted to his small phot section on the main deck, after the practice firing of HMS *King George V*'s 14-inch guns in preparation for the Allied landings in Sicily. Photo(A) Laurie Lee was called up from a successful press career, serving on board HMS *Indomitable* when she was attacked by dive-bombers in the Mediterranean in 1942 with the loss of seventy lives. Several photographers, including Photo(A) Peter Lyons, served on the extremely hazardous Russian convoys duty, taking exceptional action pictures as the convoys were bombed and torpedoed *en route*. Photo(A) Frank Bulger joined the County-class HMS *Cumberland* in September 1941, serving on her during the 'African Do' and Russian convoy escort duty.

The RAF Air Publication (1354–1936) governing photographic services for the Royal Navy had now been amended. Chapter VI on 'Air Photography in Co-operation with the Royal Navy' stated, 'As the Fleet Air Arm is an integral part of the Royal Navy, the responsibility of the Royal Air Force as regards the organisation of photographic work goes no further than the individual photographic section. Each aircraft carrier is equipped with a photographic section, the work of which is carried out by RAF personnel under the control of a suitable officer'. This is precisely the situation that Photo(A) Joe Caton found on board HMS *Ark Royal* in March 1940 when he joined the carrier alongside in Portsmouth, where she had been fitted with degaussing cables.

Joining the RN in 1936, Photo(A) Caton had seen the Admiralty Fleet Order whilst PO's mess-man on board HMS *Wolfhound*. After a first Captain's Request had refused, he was then successful in his application to transfer. When he started the course in January 1939 at Tipner, PO(Phot) Burleton was the main course instructor, assisted by LPhoto Hayward, who demonstrated close-up work on a rose in the small garden at Tipner. (Unfortunately, someone had swapped the developer with water during the exercise, with predictable results.) At the School of Air Photography at Ford, Caton and his class were digging trenches the day that war was declared. Flying experience at this time was completed in the 'Walrus' type pusher biplane, the undercarriage lock-down lever of which became the photographer's responsibility after a wheels-up landing.

Training complete, Photo(A) Caton was drafted back to Tipner as part of the photographic section, which formed a pool of photographers to meet tasking from the many agencies in the dockyard and around the Portsmouth peninsula. Particularly interesting were the experiments being carried out at this time that required photographic recording. He recalls, 'I would usually meet a Major Salter RM at Pompey Barracks and go to Southsea Beach or the Isle of Wight. He was concerned with tanks, collapsible boats and the forerunner of the amphibious DUKW vehicle (known as the "Duck")'. Twice, the photographer was required to travel to Sir Malcolm Campbell's house near Hindhead in Surrey, to photograph inventions intended to overcome beach defences including the predecessor of the 'flail' tank, used to clear minefields.

Most photographers wanted to go to sea, and eventually he was drafted to 810 Swordfish Squadron, attached to HMS *Ark Royal*. The section was run by RAF Sergeant Brandon, who, together with an RAF Leading Aircraftsman formed the nucleus of the team with the HQ photographer, Photo(A) Matthews. They were augmented by four squadron ratings as the squadrons embarked. Situated deep in the bowels of the ship above the bilges on the port side, the section was soon to be in action, but unlike other ships of the time there appear to have been no Standing Orders requiring attendance on the bridge during action stations. Routine jobs included recording deck landings, engine room defects and fuselage stress marks on the tails of the Fulmar and Swordfish aircraft which were on board. The ship sailed for the Mediterranean on what was known as a 'Club Run', meeting up with HMS *Sheffield*, HMS *Resolution* and HMS *Valiant* to form 'Force H'.

After attacks in the Mediterranean, HMS *Ark Royal* spent ninety days at sea, often sailing in and out of the Straits of Gibraltar to confuse the spies who were broadcasting their movements from La Linea across the border, and culminating in the hunt, chase and ultimate destruction of the *Bismarck*. In the Atlantic, where the *Bismarck* had been chased by RN capital ships eager to avenge the terrible fate of HMS *Hood*, the battleship was crippled by a torpedo dropped from a Swordfish of 810 Naval Air Squadron. Despite mortal wounds in the final hours of 27 May 1941, and the huge swell which caused *Ark Royal*'s deck to pitch over sixty feet, *Bismarck* continued to put up highly accurate anti-aircraft fire, which was the reason that no photographers were allowed to fly near the sinking ship. Photo(A) Caton believes that a signal was afterwards received by *Ark Royal*, critical of the lack of quality imagery from this action, which would have been of immense propaganda interest and value.

After these events, HMS *Ark Royal* ferried Hurricane fighters as close as possible to Malta, before they flew off to the defence of that beleaguered

Above:
On 9 July 1940, HMS *Ark Royal* came under heavy attack from the Italian Air Force, bombing from 14,000 feet. Carrying an F24 camera fitted with an eight-inch lens, set to 250th of a second at f8, Photo(A) Caton was standing by the after pompom guns as the bombers attacked. Deafened by the anti-aircraft fire he could not hear the bombs dropping, but focused on HMS *Hood*. He says, 'I saw the splashes start and clicked the shutter'. He succeeded in recording the best photograph of his naval career as the bombs exploded around the giant battleship.

Above:
Taken by Lieutenant Graves RNVR and processed on board HMS *Ark Royal* in 1940, this photograph shows a Fulmar fighter aircraft of 807 Naval Air Squadron passing over HMS *Renown* in the Atlantic.

island. Photo(A) Caton distinctly remembers sitting in the section aboard *Ark* below the waterline, listening to the ferocious bombing of the tanker *Ohio*, which they had escorted six hours earlier inbound for Malta. One of the few welcome respites from this action came after the ship had stopped off in Gibraltar for refuelling and the section went ashore to buy chemicals and film. When they returned with the 56lb drums of hypo developer, several bottles of rum and whisky had been placed in the bottom and were successfully hidden in an 80oz Winchester developer bottle. Jokes about drinking the developer have always abounded in the Branch, and are rooted in truth as this practice has by no means died out. Indeed, the author's vodka and Southern Comfort bottles are almost certainly still jammed in the ventilation trunking of HMS *Invincible*, empty after decanting into ordinary 5 litre plastic containers marked 'E6 First Dev'.

The 'rabbit' firm on the carrier was very healthy in 1940–41 – the section sold two thousand prints of the Mediterranean action shots on each ship. Turning over around four hundred pounds a month between four people, postcards were produced in a small easel; to alleviate the monotony of large print runs, an old money version of the service photographer's litany was recited – 'four pence, eight pence, one shilling, one shilling and four, one shilling and eight'. Due to inflation, this is now 'two pounds fifty, five pounds, seven pounds fifty, ten pounds' today, but the basic principle remains the same. Anyone who has been faced with the size of print runs needed to satisfy a ship's order will undoubtedly sympathise. Photo(A) Caton recalls: 'Of course, all this time we were still carrying on with the "rabbit" firm and after the July action had plenty of action shots to flog. One day, the Photographic Officer Lt Everitt of 820 Squadron, came storming down when we had a queue of customers because we were at the second degree of readiness!'

Being close to the bilges, the section was prone to flooding, which neatly encompasses another tribulation of the photographer – water supplies. Requiring reasonable amounts of running water to wash films and paper, naval photographers have been baling out their sections after floods at least since 1940, when Joe Caton flooded the section after attending a football match in Gibraltar. His memories will strike a chord with all those who have experienced this peculiarity of the job:

'. . . as I stepped over the 10/12″ ledge (on the hatch) I stepped in water and realised the pressure had dropped in harbour and the water was coming back through the sump. I started knocking the clips off the watertight door but realised the developing room was full up . . . I had to call the duty engineer to increase pressure . . . spoiled a hell of a lot of gear though, including some belonging to the phot officer'.

On board HMS *Albion* in 1971, the 6 Echo section was severely flooded when an ejector pump failed, and PO(Phot) Paul Yockney rang LA(Phot) Pete Craig of 848 Squadron to help clear up. He walked into the office dressed in goggles, schnorkel and flippers. In 1993 a serious flood occurred on HMS *Ark Royal* after engineers working on the water pressure inadvertently left a tap open, filling the whole section with water which ran out of the emergency egress panel in the door. HMS *Invincible* did not escape in 1994, when chemicals poured down the sink corroded the copper joint elbows, causing almost daily floods until they were replaced by plastic pipework.

Such floods are sometimes not limited to ships. LA(Phot) Richard Thompson had a burst pipe in his section at Sarajevo, Bosnia, whilst working for UNPROFOR (United Nations Protection Force) during 1995. Water temperature is often a problem on ships too, as the developer needs to be closely monitored to prevent reticulation (cracking of the emulsion on the negative caused by thermal shock). After joining HMS *Fearless* in 1991 as she came out of refit, LA(Phot) Coombs experienced much difficulty processing films at the optimum temperature of 20°C as the water was too cold. When he requested hot water, he was offered a kettle by the sympathetic Naval Stores personnel. In contrast, on HMS *Liverpool* off Monserrat during the 1997 volcanic eruptions, the water was 32°C out of the tap.

Acting PO(Phot) Louis O'Doherty took over from Flight Sergeant Brandon on board HMS *Ark Royal* in late 1940, joining the ship under the great shear leg crane in Gibraltar. The 'milk run' task in the Mediterranean continued as the demand for Hurricane fighters to defend Malta dictated, with the carrier established into a routine of deliveries' during the week and alongside in Gibraltar when not required. As the only carrier in the Mediterranean, HMS *Ark Royal* had a great propaganda as well as logistic role, which made it a prime target for the Axis forces surrounding Gibraltar. PO(Phot) O'Doherty recalls the fateful day that the carrier was torpedoed by U-81 at 1541 GMT on the 13 November 1942;

'I was having a cup of tea in the FAA CPO's and PO's Mess, just underneath the flight deck, dressed in my best uniform (PO's badges with "square rig" – as an "acting" PO) ready to go ashore in Gibraltar. The ship was conducting ADDLs – aircraft deck landing exercises – as we got closer to "the Rock", when suddenly there was a hell of a bang which knocked me to the deck. When I got up, I was walking downhill. I went uphill straight to my locker, to collect a few things I had prepared "just in case" – a few quid in a "french letter" and a HP sauce bottle full of Navy Rum. On the flight deck, I met a good oppo of mine, a wardroom steward, who had left his false teeth below, so he was wandering around all "gummy". The destroyer HMS *Legion* pulled up alongside us, so we slid down the side of the ship with fire hoses onto hammocks laid out on the foc'sle. When I got on the deck of the *Legion*, the crew commented on how smart I was.

Only one man was lost during the abandon ship, and the survivors spent the night on board HMS *Argus* in Gibraltar before returning to the UK. LPhoto(A) Hutchinson of the *Ark*'s section was particularly lucky, having also survived the sinking of HMS *Courageous* in 1939, unlike the five hundred and eighteen crew members who perished in the Atlantic.

Left:
Photographers were also attached to some of the most hazardous duties of the Second World War – convoy and escort duties to resupply Russia. Working in harsh conditions, with negligible chances of survival if sunk, they brought back some of the most unusual imagery of the war at sea. On board HMS *Scylla* in February 1943, sailors are pictured using steam jets to clear ice accretions from anchor chains and winches. If ice had been allowed to accumulate, the extra topweight could have caused the vessel to capsize.

Admiralty Press Photographers (APOs) were often civilian press photographers, directly conscripted later in the War and tasked to record any events of interest on board for the Admiralty. An outstanding example of personal dedication and bravery was exhibited by Sub-Lieutenant Charles Morgan RNVR, wounded by shrapnel on 9 April 1942, as HMS *Hermes* sunk beneath his feet after devastating attacks from the Japanese. During the attacks he remained on deck, continuing to record the scene until the slope of the deck became impossible to stand on. His account of these events is of compelling interest and merits reproduction at length. After the order was given to abandon ship:

'I took the opportunity to get a few photographs of any visible damage so quickly made my way for'ard, satisfying myself with a quick shot here and there. I worked my way to the after end, stopping amidships to get an excellent picture of a sailor sliding down the deck backwards, making an amusing shot amongst such tragic circumstances. My last picture I managed to take from right astern showing the full flight deck and superstructure with the hills of Ceylon on the horizon.'

Right:
The astonishing bravery of the Admiralty Press Photographer Sub-Lt Charles Morgan is outlined in the text, but his photographs still exercise the imagination today. The last few men to survive the sinking of HMS *Hermes* are seen here leaving the flight deck as the ship is about to roll over and sink. The photographer left the ship from the starboard (higher) side ten minutes after taking this picture, which is the second-from-last and best of the unique sequence.

'The bombers had started another attack and were diving down. Without a second's delay I opened my camera, plucked out the film and was over the side. Down, down I went in the water, my mind still thinking of that diving plane. As I started the upward journey I felt the water close around me with terrific force and, as I broke surface, pieces of shrapnel were falling quite close to me, too close to be safe. [When rescued by the hospital ship *Vita* six hours later] We all looked a sorry sight, covered from head to foot in thick black oil. I tied a piece of cloth around my body and made a complete search of the ship trying to find the other two photographers from my ship but in vain. They had perished in our gallant little ship'.

When the film was processed the images were intact although damaged by salt water. Released in 1945, they were hailed by the British press as 'some of the greatest pictures of World War Two'.

Another Admiralty Press Officer, Lt Horace Abrahams RNVR, had the galling experience of losing his priceless pictures of HMS *Prince of Wales* being sunk by the Japanese on 10 December 1941, when his own ship HMS *Repulse* was sunk directly afterwards. Attacked by eighty-four torpedo-bombers off Malaya, the two capital ships had no air cover of their own and were swiftly dispatched by the Japanese, who could not believe the lack of fighter cover. RAF Buffalo air cover was available but was not requested, as the battleships were under wireless silence and changed their plans for tactical reasons without informing the Command ashore. Lt Abrahams later recounted:

'When the order came to abandon ship, I knew I could not keep afloat because of the weight of the camera and metal slides. I placed the camera and unexposed slides in a empty steel lifeboat locker near a pompom gun on the main deck (some of the gun crew were dead) and took the slides containing pictures of the action with me when I went over the side. There were a few wits – "See you in Singapore mate" and "Now you can draw the dole". I slipped down the ship's side until I was on the protruding bulge, but as I saw one of these gaping, jagged holes made by a torpedo, I walked further aft on the beam and then went in the sea. As I came to the surface I saw a man jumping from the deck above – he had hobnailed boots on and must have been a Royal Marine. He hit me hard, split my Mae West and closed one eye. I came to the surface minus the camera slides and lost sight of the man who had hit me amongst hundreds of bobbing heads all black with fuel oil'.

Despite this experience, Lieutenant Abrahams became a Keystone Press Agency photographer in Japan after the War.

Photographers were widely employed throughout the UK in support tasks. Critical to the completion of these tasks was the introduction of the WRNS, the first course of which began training in spring 1941 at Ford. Their three-month course required no initial interest in photography, consisting of a short sharp practical introduction and drafting. Despite antipathy from some of the older ratings, manifested particularly in exclusion from 'rabbit' work, by all accounts the WRNS were a lively and welcome addition to the Branch, fulfilling their intended role of freeing men for active service.

Below:
Illustrated magazine of 27 March 1943 carried this article, featuring many of the Wrens whose recollections have been incorporated into this history. Verity Waterlow and Kathleen Graham of the second course (left), practising interior photography in Climping Church near Ford (right).

WRENS
and the Lens

PHOTOGRAPHY is one of the jobs undertaken by Wrens, thus releasing more naval men for sea-going duties.

At a special course the girls are trained in the use of every kind of camera and photographic equipment, including the technique of aerial photography. For this purpose they are flown over selected areas to take their pictures from the air.

In the picture on the left, Wren photographers are returning with results of their first photographic flight during training at the Royal Naval School of photography.

The theory of photography is also studied in class, and theory is put to practice locally as, right, the girls photograph a church under the direction of a naval instructor.

These girls will be posted to naval stations to take over work as photographic assistants in all parts of the country where their work will be most valuable.

Left:
The WRNS made an important contribution to the Branch during the War. Spared the RNSOP at Tipner, all WRNS completed training at Ford, Sussex in 1942, where the second qualifying course is seen (left) with the Commander of the School of Photography (centre right) and the Chief Petty Officer instructor (centre left). Molly Chapman, the Wren of 'fudge in developer trays' fame (extreme right), appears to be holding a half-plate dark slide, indicating that the photograph was probably taken by an S4 ground camera.

Above:
Wrens often ended up undertaking much of the darkroom work in sections, becoming proficient in dodging, shading and other techniques. This set-up publicity picture was taken on 19 January 1942 at RNAS Donibristle, the Naval Air Station close to the mighty Firth of Forth bridge in Scotland.

Above:
Unusually shot in colour by the press photographer Wilf Cross, this shot was widely disseminated for public relations. Conscripted as Photo(A) Cross, the photographer was known as 'one-shot' Wilf for his ability to achieve the task first time. Women rarely flew in the Branch, but were occasionally allowed to test the F24 camera. Wren Pat Gould went on to become a Torpedo Assessing Officer, analysing films from the P39 Torpedo Practice cameras.

Complementing section work generally, some also brought an unusual femine touch to the Branch, including fudge made in developer trays and underwear in the rotary glazing machines. Several ladies achieved promotion to Petty Officer and moved on to instruct classes of WRNS or assess aerial photography. Although there must have been some two hundred women trained as photographers during hostilities, most of the Branch were unaware of their existence as they completed their task without fuss.

The Aircraft Recognition Centre (ARC) at Yeovilton had a large staff of WRNS, helping to produce the huge amount of posters that were required, showing all types of enemy aircraft for instruction purposes. Typical tasking included model recording from all aspects against sky/cloud backdrops to assist recognition, matching pairs of aircraft and most aircraft crews were photographed and held on file in case they were lost in action or distinguished themselves. Camouflage trials were also conducted by photographing equipment from various altitudes to reveal their degrees of visibility to the enemy.

In 1941, the Fleet Requirements Unit was formed, primarily to supply the fleet with qualified people for rapid deployment. Photographers were supplied to this pool after extra flying experience with 35mm Newman Sinclair cine cameras, plus basic instruction on navigation and wireless telegraphy, for which they received extra pay.

This task involved the dangerous marking of gunnery shoots from the air, flying in outdated and obsolete Blackburn Roc and Skua aircraft. Fitted for towing a drogue, the target was deployed from the aircraft by a 1000-yard cable where it would be engaged by the ship. The long-suffering photographer would view the shell bursts through a Perspex 'rake', marked with boxes corresponding to degrees of displacement of the shot from the drogue. The reading would be called to the Air Gunner for recording and subsequent analysis. For air-to-surface work, photographic recording of the bursts was undertaken using the 35mm cine Newman Sinclair or the F24 aerial camera, which required close passes to record direct hits. Hazardously standing up in the open cockpit with the large camera, Photo(A) Tom Hawkes was often thrown in the air on the end of the harness when the aircraft hit airpockets. Photo(A) Francis Saunders also flew over 450 hours doing this type of work, which was normally piloted by trainee aircrew. He lost count of the number of times he had to sit as a helpless passenger as the new pilot flew the traditional dangerous 'initiation' between the old Man of Hoy rock formation and the cliffs of the Orkney Islands.

Dive-bombing practice was required in the Skua, which was the first operational naval dive-bomber in service. However, the aircraft was underpowered, which made an early pull-up after bomb release essential. The Newman Sinclair was used for marking these runs, mounted on a board across the cockpit offset at fifteen degrees. Photo(A) Saunders recalls one particular incident:

'As you went into the dive, you started the camera going . . . On one occasion, dive-bombing the stern of a ship on exercises . . . as we went over it the aircraft shook and put the wind up me for a minute. I asked the pilot if he had felt the vibration, he said he had, but it was only the hot air from the ship. When we got back I looked around the kite, and on the port wing the Light Series bomb racks were missing. A few days later, the Commanding Officer had a parcel arrive at his office – it contained the bomb racks in quite a mangled condition. Accompanying them was a note, which read "Please instruct your crews not to litter my decks in future".'

Two photographers were killed undertaking this hazardous duty, Photo(A) Strachan after his aircraft failed to pull out during a dive-bombing exercise on Caril Beach, and LPhoto(A) Spiller whose aircraft ditched after an engine failure whilst recording a gunnery shoot. They are respectively buried in Crail Church, Fife and Kirkwall Church, Orkney.

Also in 1941, on the night of Friday 10 January, the RN School of Photography and the RN Gas School at Tipner were hit by a single bomb, believed to have been off target from the main attacks directed at Portsmouth. The thin wooden huts were badly damaged by the blast and although training continued this event must have further concentrated intentions to move the school to an airstation.

Gunnery analysis remained essential, and advances were incorporated in

the fleet as soon as practicable with wartime urgency. The need for several ships to conduct practice firings against the same target simultaneously resulted in the introduction of Dufaycolour filters and transparency film in 1942, which could record the coloured dyes used in the shells. Maintaining the theme of meeting gunnery needs as they arose, in 1943 a Mobile Analysis and Recording Unit was established in two converted motor coaches, formed to analyse the gunnery of 'Hunt' class destroyers. Weapons trials for HMS *Vernon* took place at the Aircraft Torpedo Development Unit, located at Stokes Bay in Alverstoke, where a special camera on the end of the pier produced strip images of the weapon leaving the aircraft and falling. These were stuck together to form one picture, giving a clear indication of weapon drop performance.

Also during 1943, the Admiralty finally acted to close the anomaly in regulations that had allowed servicemen to make a great deal of money by selling exclusive pictures to the press. This had become a significant security problem, and was a loophole that had allowed individuals to claim copyright to the detriment of the Service. Conversely, due to the insidious encroachment of European legislation into the Navy of the 1990s, the position on copyright is now far less defined and still awaits legal ratification, as the RN currently maintains the probably indefensible position of claiming 'commissioning' copyright for the Crown.

With the intention of moving closer to the Fleet Air Arm at RNAS Ford, the RNSOP moved permanently to Bognor Regis in 1943, housed in commandeered houses on the seafront at Felpham. The main school was situated in Strand House, the home of the financier Clarence Hattray (reputedly responsible for the Wall Street Crash of 1929) with several other large houses in the locality acting as outstations. Strand House served as the HQ of the school, until burnt out in 1944 by a V1 doodlebug. Flying experience for trainees was conducted from Cowdray Park, Tangmere and RAF Ford as appropriate. One photographer at the time remembers, 'The heavy F24 camera used for this task had a neck strap, so if you dropped it you went with it; saving you the worry of having to pay for it'. He also clearly recalls a Squadron Commander's brief to his aircrew about photographers, 'Phots are the ones with brown fingers and concertinas on their arms'. The arm badge has now changed.

Once the tide of war had turned, preparations for the invasion of France began with much secrecy. After signing the Official Secrets Act, a small party of photographic ratings including WRNS was sent to the New Bodelian Library at Oxford, loaned to MI6 after a massive nation-wide appeal by the BBC for holiday pictures of the coast of France. These pictures were copied with an F24 camera and motor drive, processed, and over one thousand prints made from each negative. Assembled sequentially in scrapbooks for briefings, these images were annotated by MI6 foreign operatives, visiting the unit after being met from Oxford Station by the team. The whole operation was highly classified due to the obvious invasion target, and attracted many VIPs and Senior Command staff. Printing one day, Photo(A) Saunders

Above:
During the severe night attacks of 10 January 1941, Portsmouth was heavily bombed. One bomb, believed to be a stray from a stick aimed at HMS *Excellent*, landed at the school, causing considerable damage. This panorama, taken from the roof of the Film Studio, shows the destruction. Unfortunately, the motorway precludes a direct comparison view today.

Above:
This picture of a Wren photographer, receiving the camera from a Walrus 'pusher' biplane at HMS *Daedalus*, acts as a reminder that the Branch also supported the aircraft and aircrew by processing film and loading camera magazines. Indeed, the section on board HMS *Illustrious* in 1944 lost a camera when the observer who had borrowed it was shot down during an attack on the *Tirpitz* in the Norwegian fjords.

Right:
Shore-based photographers were tasked to record important events that occurred in their units, and were therefore in attendance for divisions, presentations and other ceremonial occasions. This previously unpublished image shows the touching moment when the survivors of the sunken HMS *Ark Royal*, including PO(Phot) Louis O'Doherty, were marched onto the quarterdeck at HMS *Daedalus*, receiving the cheers of the assembled Ship's Company. A Wren photographer may be seen (extreme left) on the fence, recording the scene from the other end of the line.

Above:
The combination of VIPs and British naval might produced some evocative opportunities for photography. Visiting the Home Fleet in February 1943, King George V walks beneath the guns of HMS *Howe* at Scapa Flow, accompanied by Captain C. Woodhouse (left) and Admiral Sir John Tovey (right).

Right:
Occasionally, the Service photographer produces work that transcends the mundane recording and becomes a record of a society and a time. The carefully controlled depth of field, pin sharp on the face of the prisoner, focuses attention on his captive plight and produces a most disturbing effect. This blindfolded survivor of U-boat U489, sunk by a Sunderland flying boat of 423 Sqn RCAF on 4 August, is helped ashore from HMS *Orwell* at Greenock on 11 August 1943.

became aware of a party of visitors, and stood back to allow them to see the image on the baseboard. As he stepped back, he stood on someone's foot, but nothing was said until the Petty Officer in charge came back after the visit. 'That was General Wavell's foot you stood on,' he said.

The equipment and personnel build-up for D-Day in the Solent area was recorded by naval photographers from HMS *Daedalus*. One photographer recalls that 'the troops would always ask if they were off today', indicating the security of the actual date was well kept even in the secure coastline areas.

Whilst developments continued at home, the photographers trained at Tipner had now been widely dispersed through the fleet, and some quality imagery had begun to percolate through the censor to newspapers and magazines, as seen in the following examples.

THE FAR EAST

Reconnaissance had always been an important aspect of the Service photographer's task, but the likelihood of further conflict against the Japanese resulted in a significant new photographic development, the formation of the Fleet Air Arm's only dedicated Photo-Reconnaissance Unit. The specific idea of Lord Louis Mountbatten, when Supreme Allied Commander of South East Asia, 88 Naval Air Squadron was formed on 10 June 1944, primarily to obtain beach surveys, tide data and gradient information for Operation *Zipper*, the invasion of Malaya. Based at HMS *Bherunda* on Colombo Racecourse, the squadron deployed its six sky-blue PR Grumman Hellcats to various units of the East Indies Fleet as required for the task, including HMS *Indefatigable* in early 1945 and HMS *Emperor* in April. Flying without any armament at extreme altitude over the target area for several hours, these operations were the longest (7–8 hours) and highest (27,000–36,000 feet) undertaken by the Fleet Air Arm in unpressurised aircraft during the War. Fitted with American K17 9″ × 9″ cameras with six-inch lenses, and K18 9″ × 18″ cameras with 24-inch lenses, the squadron had no less than fifteen photographers attached to ensure loading, processing and mosaic laying progressed smoothly.

During the recce for Operation *Zipper*, Sub-Lt (A) J.W. Thomlinson RNVR suffered engine failure over the target, and successfully got ashore near Port Swettenham where he was captured by the Japanese. On 20 July 1945 he was beheaded on a hill to the north of Pasir Pajang, Singapore – a typically barbaric and revolting atrocity which contributed to the unusual tide of personal hatred running in the fleet at this time against the Japanese. The invasion of Malaya was set for 9 September 1945 and the recce for this operation was complete. Then the Americans unveiled 'the destroyer of worlds' to the Japanese and ended the War. When 888 Squadron's task became public, their contribution to the aborted invasion of Malaya was reported in the South East Asia Command newspaper, couched in the typical prose of the time:

> 'The "Top Secret" story of 888 Squadron, Royal Navy, can now be told – how it took the photographs from which the maps for the invasion of Malaya were made. Over 100,000 square miles of Siam, Malaya and Sumatra were photographed. The hazards of this flying, many miles from the carriers in single-engined aircraft, were great. Processing the negatives was done in the carriers at sea.'

The Commanding Officer of the squadron, Senior Pilot and senior Petty Officer (Photographer) were decorated before the squadron disbanded in August 1946, leaving behind an enduring cartographic legacy; much of their quality work forming the basis for mapping the colony post-war.

The Japanese finally capitulated on 2 September 1945, after the Americans had dropped the second nuclear bomb on Nagasaki. This much debated event saved many months of war and the lives of thousands of servicemen who would otherwise have perished.

One photographer, Photo(A) Raymond Wingate, was sent straight from the photographic course to HMS *Commonwealth* at Kure in Japan, where he

Below:
Unique in the history of the Fleet Air Arm, 888 NAS were the only dedicated photo-reconnaissance squadron ever commissioned. The Commanding Officer, Lt-Cdr (A) Brian Macaw DSC RNVR, is seen here in the cockpit of a Hellcat at Colombo Racecourse (HMS *Bherunda*), Ceylon in August 1945. Note the markings under the cockpit, depicting a camera over the 'Rising Sun' Japanese flag, which indicate the successful completion of ten photo-recce missions.

Below:
The importance and size of the reconnaissance task allocated to this squadron demanded significant

photographic support, to which no less than fifteen photographers were drafted. Fitting and testing an eclectic mix of RAF and USAF cameras, depending on the lens length and format required, three phots manhandle a typical selection back to the aircraft line from the workshop, situated in the grandstand of Colombo Racecourse.

On the left, Photo (A) Cyril Long holds an RAF type F52 with a 36-inch lens, capable of taking 500 exposures, In the centre, Photo (A) Albert Cliffe carries an American service model K18, fitted with a 24-inch lens for a large scale intelligence cover onto a 9˝x18˝ negative format. Finally, on the right is Photo (A) Peter Stappenbeck, a K18 on his shoulder and a K17 survey camera (6-inch lens) in his left hand.

Right:

Despite the great battle to ultimate victory being fought in Europe, the implacable Japanese foe still awaited in the East. Many photographers from RNSOP at Tipner were sent straight to the Far East, as the British reinforced for the long struggle ahead. HMS *Valiant* and FS *Richelieu* lie under the guns of HMS *Queen Elizabeth*, the flagship of the Commander-in-Chief, Eastern Fleet.

Above:

In recognition of the critical role to be played by aircraft carriers against the Japanese, a large number were built on former merchant hulls in America, commissioned and sent as 'Woolworth's escort carriers to the Far East theatre. The squadron photographers attached to 807 Naval Air Squadron, embarked in HMS *Hunter*, pose on deck by a Seafire aircraft of the unit, accompanied by their Photographic Officer.

Right middle:

As the war in the Far East continued, the benefits of conscripting civilian press photographers became apparent. This timeless shot was taken by an Admiralty photographer on board the flagship of the Far East Fleet in April 1944.

Right:

On 2 September 1945 the capitulation of Japan was signed on board the battleship USS *Missouri*. Shortly afterwards, the Japanese military commanders on the various fronts of war surrendered in a series of ceremonies. Sub-Lt Douglas Rendell attended one of these events, held on board HMS *Nelson* off Penang, and remembers 'a mass of photographers squashed up against the bulkhead to record the proceedings'. He later attended the surrender of the Japanese in South East

was fortunate to be seconded to the forces newspaper, *British Commonwealth Occupation News*. Wearing his square rig and bell bottoms, he was allowed complete autonomy, and therefore became the first British Forces photographer in Hiroshima, taking some of the early scenes of devastation later featured in the famous book *Hiroshima* by John Hersey. Photo(A) Wingate recalled:

'Do you remember seeing the spokes of a bicycle burnt into the tarmac at Hiroshima. That was one of mine and was published all over the place. Never got a penny, though, as it was an official naval photograph.'

These graphic yet historic images of devastation are still on display at the Peace Park Memorial in Hiroshima today.

Asia, accepted by Lord Louis Mountbatten in Singapore on 12 September. Every photographer in the area descended upon Singapore and at the parade through the town a great variety of cameras could be seen – including the RN F24. A branch character, Willy Bence, was in Singapore for the surrender, using a Watson stand camera and trays of flash powder. After the picture was taken, a cloud of soot descended on the assembled dignitaries – all dressed in white tropical dress uniform.

Below:
HMS *Glory* was the venue chosen for the Japanese surrender of Rabaul. On Sept 6 1945, the section on board photographed the Japanese General Imamura and his line of staff officers queuing on the flight deck to surrender their swords. Recorded on glass plates and annotated by the photographer concerned, many other original glass negatives of this type lie decaying and ruined in the storage vault at the Surface Flotilla Photographic Unit (SFPU).

Above left:
Although in poor condition, at least the negatives of the surrender of Rabaul have survived. The same cannot be said for Photo(A) Raymond Wingate's priceless pictures of Hiroshima, exposed on glass plates when he was attached to HMS *Commonwealth* in Kure, Japan. Copy prints are readily available from many sources, but the original negatives have been stolen, presumably for their high commercial value. Important historical negatives like this should be safeguarded by the Royal Navy.

Left:
'Who would have thought I would have finished up doing that from Felpham?' The first British Forces photographer into Hiroshima, Photo(A) Wingate was allowed to wander around the devastated city, taking high quality images that are today displayed around the world.

THE ROYAL NAVAL FILM SECTION

Above:
Established in 1939 under the administrative umbrella of the RNSOP, the FN Film Section conscripted experienced film people to make instructional films. Seen here on set is part of the section, with director of photography Gordon Dynes (top), discussing the next step whilst cameraman Martin Curtis awaits (seated by the Vinten camera). Stanley Cousins (extreme left) holds the script for the shoot.

Above:
Elements of the film unit were detached for D-Day. (Specific tasks are outlined in the main text.) Lt Gordon Dynes and Petty Officer Martin Curtis were required to produce a complete film of the Arromanches 'Mulberry' harbour, from D-Day itself to the completion of the enterprise. Towards the end of the task, on 17 June 1944, Lt Gordon Dynes (left) examines the Newman Sinclair cine camera on the beach, while PO Curtis holds the 'Royal Navy Combat Film Unit' clapper board. The completed 'Mulberry' harbour stretches away behind them.

Whilst the still photography side of the Branch had been thus engaged, the need for motion pictures to show the Royal Navy's view of events and to provide practical training material had led to the formation of the Royal Navy Film Unit (RNFU). The RNFU was formed in 1939 by Lt-Cdr Penn Tennyson RNVR, formerly the youngest and most promising director from Ealing Film studios, and established under the administrative command of Commander (G) G.V.A. Phelips RN in the purpose-built studio and processing laboratory complex at Tipner.

The unit possessed an extraordinary array of talent, conscripted from the Crown Film Unit, Ministry of Information and feature film studios. All aspects of motion picture production were covered, from separate film / sound recording to dubbing, cutting (editing) and animation, with the aim of producing complete documentary and instructional films in-house. Cameras, projectors and sound production equipment were obtained from America as part of Lend Lease in late 1942, and for some time the RNFU was the most up-to-date unit in the UK. This large film team included the resident director John Paddy Carstairs (who made comedy films after the War), cameramen Gordon Dynes, Martin Curtis, Ernie Stewart and Roly Stafford, and the cutting team of 3rd Officer WRNS Hazel Wilkinson with five Leading Hands, including Joe Mendoza who was later to have a successful career directing documentary films. Another interesting rating conscript to join the unit was 'Paddy' Vinten, of the famous optical company. As a rating photographer, 'Paddy' had to be given a travel warrant every month to attend company board meetings. The sound side of motion picture making was under the control of Lt-Cdr 'Ching' Mountenay. The ninety-strong animation team, based in the balloon hut on Range Green, provided the huge amount of animation cell 'trace and paint' for the many training films made.

The RNFU was a showpiece, visited by many VIPs. Productions included a series of instructional films on rocket projectors, which helped the Russians develop their famous 'Katusha' battlefield system, as well as a series on each of the specialisations in the Fleet Air Arm. The security advantages of in-house production came to the fore during the preparations for invasion in 1944, and much secret work was undertaken, including the production of instructional material on the assembly of the 'Mulberry' harbour for D-Day and training films for two-man submarine operators. The editing was supervised by MI5, who sat over the cutters and picked up every sprocket dropped during the process.

Secret trials of invasion equipment were filmed, assessing its reliability prior to the event in the expected adverse weather conditions. Large steel assemblies, known as bombardons, were designed to minimise the amplitude of the waves in the outer approaches to the artificial harbour and were filmed in rough weather in Weymouth Bay from one of the few autogyros in the country at the time. In preparation for D-Day in 1944, the animation section at Tipner was taken to RAF Nuneham Courtenay, where the famous briefing model for the 617 Squadron 'Dam Busters' raid was constructed. Here, a large model of the D-Day beaches was manufactured in small sections, for security reasons, before final assembly. A month before D-Day, four cameramen were detached to London, briefed with selected elements of the press (under armed guard), then detached to two separate ships bound for France. One team, 'Bash' Beeson and Roly Stafford, was detached to a destroyer, which was tasked with Naval Gunfire Support (NGS) for the infantry on King Red beach in Gold sector. On 6 June, the team was in action obtaining footage of HMS *Belfast* and HMS *Diadem* firing inland, and of gun positions ashore under bombardment. The other team, Gordon Dynes and Martin Curtis, was ordered to produce a full record of the 'Mulberry' harbour at Arromanches, from the first scuttling of the blockships around the site to the full assembly of the concrete caissons into an artificial habour.

Crossing the Channel in a paddle steamer from Gosport, the film team left with other specialists (demolition men etc.) in the first wave of the invasion, and the task was completed over the next six weeks. On returning to Tipner, dressed in khaki with a revolver on his hip, the first person Martin Curtis encountered was the Commander, who immediately ordered him to change into the correct rig, no matter what he had been doing. One of the RNFU's last jobs in 1945 was Operation *Tinfish*, the scuttling of surrendered U-Boats off Scotland under the overall mantle of Operation *Deadlight*. It was filmed from HMS *Onslow* by Roly Stafford and Ron Bicker.

The Film Unit was ultimately viewed as inefficient by the professional personnel conscripted to serve there, although many training films of value were made. Unhappy with the constraints imposed by the unit, many ratings actually volunteered for more active service, only to be turned down on the grounds that their work was essential. One director, Terry Bishop, was conscripted at such an inappropriate level for his experience that, whilst making a film series on the history of naval gunnery, he had to be demobilised so he could attend the Long (G) course at HMS *Excellent* (the course for Lieutenants and above). On completion of the course, which he spent living in a suite at the Queens Hotel, Southsea, he was reaccepted, given a commission and made the films. Tipner seems to have been a springboard to many, with a large number of these talented people going on to successful careers after the War in their respective fields, from the animator Digby Turpin who worked on the Beatles film *Yellow Submarine* to Paul Beeson, the cameraman who filmed many well known scenes in *The Sound of Music*. The animator Ralph Wansborough served at Tipner, as did many 'names' in fifties and sixties cinema which are less familiar today.

The following photographs depict more examples of wartime Photographic Branch work.

Above:
During the making of the instructional film *How an Aircraft Flies*, the RN Film Section required some close-up footage of an aircraft being hit with machine-gun bullets. On board HMS *Ravager* (an escort carrier working up squadrons in the Clyde) a damaged tail section was allocated to the task, and is shown here being filmed by Roly Stafford while the individual on the left engages it with a machine-gun.

Above:
The same film required footage of aircrew and cockpit shots, so the section borrowed a Supermarine Seafire, which was transported to Pinewood studio for the requisite filming sequences.

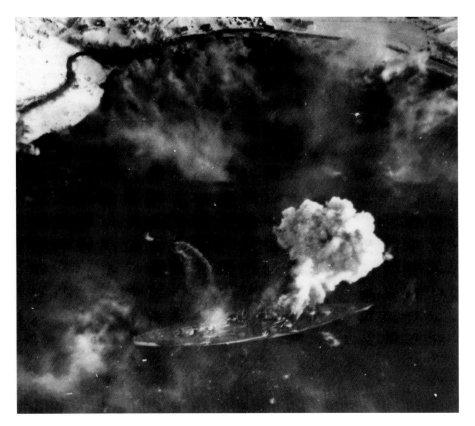

Left:
Processed on board HMS *Illustrious*, this impressive action picture of the attack on the *Tirpitz* was taken by the observer with an F24 camera in one of the Fleet Air Arm strike aircraft on 3 April 1944. Used for post-raid analysis, hundreds of images like this were produced urgently by the on board phot staff – a massive task with the primitive equipment available.

Right:
In addition to the public relations and record work undertaken, the primary task of the Branch continued in the form of gunnery analysis. Here the Eastern Fleet cruiser HMS *Newcastle* calibrates her guns on 3 April 1944, recorded by the photographic team on shore near Trincomalee.

Above:
This famous shot was taken by ship's staff on board HMS *Furious*, just before the launch of the raid on the *Tirpitz* in Alten Fjord on 3 April 1944. Armourer Bob Cotcher is seen chalking his personal message for the ship on a 1600lb bomb.

Below:
The media-conscious Churchill recognised the value of a good, newsworthy photograph, whether posing with a Tommy gun in 1940 or as here with the giant armament of HMS *Prince of Wales* whilst on the way to meet President Roosevelt in August 1941. During the voyage across the Atlantic, the Prime Minister Winston Churchill and his advisers often took to the quarterdeck to stretch their legs as part of the press calls. Recorded here by an anonymous naval photographer are (from left) General Sir J. Dill, Churchill, Mr Harry Hopkins, Admiral Sir Dudley Pound and Air Marshal Sir W. Freeman.

POST-WAR RATIONALISATION

A shortage of experienced instructors, combined with the greatly increased remit of RN photography, led to a perceived and not unexpected decrease in photographic efficiency; a state that continued throughout the War despite being alleviated to some extent by the call-up of qualified civilian photographers. By the end of the Second World War, it had become clear to the Admiralty and Fleet Air Arm that the Photographic Branch needed attention to confirm its tasking, accountability and responsibilities. Users of the Branch made a joint representation, stating that the present system was inadequate to deal with the increasing needs of the Service and poorly defined areas of responsibility. A review was therefore undertaken by the Organisation and Methods team at the Admiralty, resulting in the dissemination of AWD 1357/45 on 26 Jan 1946. This report made twenty-three separate criticisms of the system, and made it clear that Director Airfields and Carrier Requirements (DACR) staff were not assuming the lead role that was expected of them by their Terms of Reference. This report so inceased DACR, particularly as that agency had been part of the initial joint representation for improvement, that the Flag Staff wrote a step-by-step rebuttal of the twenty-three points of criticism, rightly pointing out that they had inherited a run down, poorly equipped and overloaded system on the brink of war, and had done their best with limited materials ever since.

As a result of the report, the relevant departments of the Admiralty decided to remuster the Branch to the Fleet Air Arm permanently, forming a part of the newly-formed Naval Airman specialisation. Deliberations to this effect began in 1947, hampered by the demographic problem of a number of experienced CS (Continuous Service) seaman photographic ratings who did not wish to become part of the Fleet Air Arm. Indeed, a report of 7 November 1947, from the Officer-in-Charge of RNSOP Felpham, indicated that all 7 CS ratings (2 Chief Petty Officers, 5 Petty Officers and 2 Leading Hands) at the RNSOP refused to transfer. A sensible compromise was reached, in the recognition that it was vital to retain the old specialisation to keep these experienced people. Ratings were offered the choice of becoming Naval Airman photographers, complete with new 'aeroplane' style badges and significantly enhanced advancement prospects, or remaining Photo(A)s with the old 'camera' badge and an awareness of the small chance of promotion. This change was effected at a local level throughout the fleet.

Meanwhile, the end of the War and the repeal of the many Hostilities Only regulations meant that the RNSOP houses at Felpham had to be handed back to their civilian owners. In 1947 the school moved to HMS *Peregrine* at the now Royal Naval Air Station at Ford. In September of that year, the first Volunteer (Continuous Service) course began. The school now settled down to the vastly smaller throughput required for the peacetime Navy, concentrating on Phot 2, Phot 1 training and courses for non-specialist Officers about to take up photographic appointments. Quality and standards were not neglected, with the 1951 Petty Officer's course under Lt 'Freddie' Rodgers qualifying Phot 1 trainees for exemption from examination at Intermediate level with the Institute of Incorporated Photographers (IIP), the forerunner of the British Institute of Professional Photography. Special National Service courses were also arranged, and were perceived as good deals for those ratings who joined, as they were trained to a high standard and sent straight into civilian employment after service. Successful public relations efforts were made to inform civilians of the workings and abilities of the Branch. These included Phot 1's advanced career course ratings being

Below:
Transfer to the reconstituted Naval Airman branch reflected the increased importance of photographic services to the Fleet Air Arm. Naval photographer T. Weathers reloads the vertical F24 camera on a Sea Fury of 739 Squadron, HMS *Hornbill* at RNAS Culham in 1948.

Below:
The world cruise undertaken by King George VI and the Royal Family in 1947 held particular significance, being the first tour undertaken since the Second World War. Embarking on 1 February in Portsmouth Dockyard, the King takes the salute from the Captain of the mighty battleship HMS *Vanguard*, attended by the Queen and the young princesses, Elizabeth and Margaret.

sent to Alexandra Palace with the BBC on acquaint and magazine articles in the civilian press. The principal equipment in use at this time included the ever faithful half plate Watson stand camera, the 9cm × 12cm Van Neck press camera, the Newman Sinclair cine camera and the '8308' enlarger.

One particular National Serviceman photographer distinguished himself in 1955 on board HMS *Eagle*, making a superb film of the crash of a Wyvern aircraft that became a standard initial brief for flight deck personnel. A young pilot was experiencing difficulty in landing the unwieldy Wyvern on deck, making several approaches before literally crashing directly into the funnel. The cine film from the top of the Flying Control position was dramatic as at one stage the aircraft headed straight for the camera, even showing the pilot falling out of the cockpit whilst still in his ejection seat. The stills photographer took pictures so quickly that he sheared a pin in the K20 camera. The cine photographer received a Commander-in-Chief's commendation for this work.

Right:
Photographers on trials ships and carriers performed the valuable task of cine filming each launch and recovery. These films were analysed for evidence in the event of an accident. Trainee aircrew on trials, working up in very powerful piston-engined aircraft on ships for the first time, made for interesting but very hazardous work. On 25 May 1949, NA(Phot) Paul Johnson captured Sea Fury VR941 upside-down on HMS *Illustrious*. The pilot was trapped until he was released by the flight deck rating seen running in from the left.

Below:
The film *Above Us the Waves* used the expertise of naval divers to assist in the production of underwater sequences. Sir John Mills, Donald Sinden and James Robertson Justice led the cast for this film, which was an account of an unrelenting British attack on a Nazi warship. In this typical 'internal PR shot', the RN diving team pose with Sir John Mills (centre) after the underwater shooting at Portland Naval Base in Dorset. Petty Officer Diver Peter Barrett is second from right.

The provision of photographic services to the fleet now settled into a routine, with photographers dispersed throughout the Service, from aircraft carriers to squadron photographers on helicopter and fixed-wing units. Shore-based sections provided support to their parent establishments, and secret work calibrating submarine periscope cameras was undertaken by specially trained ratings. The Royal Navy was still a large and impressive organisation, providing a variety of tasking. The cine filming of each aircraft launch and recovery was always required, although the films had no value unless an incident occurred. Trials ships also used specialist equipment to measure take-off, landing speed and undercarriage (oleo) sink rate. The 'end speed' cameras used were similar to racecourse cameras, recording the exact speed that the aircraft took the arrester wires on deck by measuring the length of the image on the film. Finally, a growing awareness of the importance of public relations work can be traced to this time.

Of course, wherever the action was the Branch was not far behind. HMS *Ocean* was tasked to drop troops off for the Malayan emergency in 1949, and on the way through the Suez the section photographed military installations for intelligence purposes, a wise precaution in the light of future events. During this deployment Lt Riddams RN, the Photographic Officer on board, was tragically killed in a Firefly crash whilst orbiting the ship conducting a photographic sortie.

The section ratings on board HMS *Ocean* processed reconnaissance film during the Korean War, and on several occasions were required to fly over hostile territory in the back of a Firefly, recording obliques of target damage with the F24 camera. Processing was done by inspection with a safelight, modified as required by the weather experienced over the target area. Thin negatives could be stained with pyrogallic acid to make them more dense. During the Korean War, LA(Phot) 'Geordie' Penman and his Photographic Officer had the unpleasant experience of being taken prisoner when their base at Chodo was overrun by the Chinese, spending two years in captivity before the end of hostilities.

As the Fleet Photographer based in Hong Kong PO(Phot) Dave King was ordered to film the shelling of terrorist positions in Malaya during 1956. However, the 5.25-inch guns of HMNZS *Royalist* blew the phot team off the director top, gunsmoke obscured the view of the cameras and when the film was processed in the only receptable large enough on board (the Captain's bath) the chemicals stained the bath. PO(Phot) King was consequently put on a disciplinary charge. Another successful day in the Photographic Branch. Other duties in Hong Kong included intelligence work photographing the Warsaw Pact/Chinese ship's registration papers, a task which required the photographer to change into civilian clothes, collect a half plate camera disguised as golf gear and meet the ship on arrival. Given one minute exactly to photograph the documents, the 'golfer' would often walk past the Ship's Captain on completion of his job with no questions ever being asked. Towards the end of the year, HMS *Eagle* alongside in Gibraltar was suddenly required to sail and assist in the Suez operation, the photographic section once again processing the essential reconnaissance film and G45 16mm cine from the Sea Hawk fighters.

Back home, staff work continued on Branch matters, marked by the release of the new Book of Reference (BR 870–2) which was designed to clarify the task of the specialisation. It stated:

'The photographic organisation of the Royal Navy is provided for:
(a) Operational purposes
(b) Surveys
(c) Recording and analysis of practices and exercises
(d) Instruction and training
(e) Technical assessment and records
(f) Historical record
(g) Photographic publicity'

The first clear statements relevant to the importance of public relations were also outlined:

'It is Admiralty policy, for recruiting and morale purposes, as well as to let the taxpayer know what the Navy is doing with his money, to fulfil as far as possible all requests from sources for publicity photographs and to stimulate interest by supplying material which seems worthy of publication'.

In a throwback to the Second World War, the Phot 1 course at RNAS Ford in 1959 was still being instructed in topographical modelling, making the Isle of Wight in sections for the instructor, Bert Sinfield. This model had been at least ten years in the making, because one of the courses back in 1949 had constructed 'the Needles' cliffs for it! Drinking practice off duty took place in the 'Arundel Arms' local pub, known as the 'Shaky Do' due to the thriving black market and credited with helping ratings to achieve the traditional high alcohol tolerance required for the trade. Trainee photographers flew in Auster aircraft to gain air experience, while the school continued to routinely produce well-trained ratings for the fleet. RNAS Ford also boasted an equipment trials section. The newly commissioned Sub-Lt Paul Johnson tested kit for the fleet, severely criticising some items that were unsuited for the peculiar requirements of naval service.

This section were deeply involved with the secret work on 'Trial Victor', designed to test the fusing mechanism of the new Sea Slug missile. Operating only in the worst weather conditions at HMS *Cambridge*, the fuse was test fired on a six-inch shell at low trajectory to measure interference. The projectile was photographically recorded in flight.

Due to the imminent closure of RNAS Ford in 1961, the RNSOP moved again, this time to Whitecroft House at HMS *Daedalus* while a new school

Above:
Prince Philip completed a distinguished naval career, including wartime service, before being 'permanently detached' to the Royal Family. In autumn 1949, he was serving as the First Lieutenant of HMS *Chequers*, attached to HMS *St Angelo* in Malta as the leader of the First Mediterranean Destroyer Flotilla. Princess Elizabeth visited him during this period of duty, posing for this picture with the Staff Officers of HMS *St Angelo*.

Above:
Many tasks of the Branch have hardly changed down the years. At parades and other formal occasions, photographers have the envied ability to walk around taking pictures, instead of being 'fell in' with the other men. Suppliers of limelight to the Senior Officers of the Navy, there are several true stories about photographers who simply fire the flash regularly during visits without loading any film, as most visits are stultifyingly boring. This can, however, go badly wrong if the officer requests a particular shot – time for a technical excuse. Photo(A) Ray Bromelow, on the left, covers a Flag Officer's visit at Lossiemouth during 1954.

Above :
The light fleet aircraft carrier HMS *Centaur* (RO6) prepares to enter harbour on 27 April 1955, with her full complement of twelve Sea Fury FB11s and six Avenger AS4 aircraft ranged on deck. Photographing a warship's entry into harbour is a fascinating task, giving a wide scope of opportunities as the ship manoeuvres with her complement and air group on deck.

Above right:
Aircraft carrier service inevitably required the accurate recording of aircraft trials, which occasionally could go wrong with a speed only understood by those who have served on flight decks. On the fleet carrier HMS *Eagle* in 1949, this Westland HR3 Dragonfly WG708 appears to have lifted from the deck while still attached to the towing and manoeuvring arm, which has swung back and struck the tail rotor. This has detached, causing loss of control and resulting in the death of the pilot. Accurate photographic records of these sad events allows detailed preventative analysis for flight safety.

Right:
At 19:37 GMT on 15 May 1957, Britain detonated the country's first hydrogen bomb at Christmas Island in the Indian Ocean, testing the radiation implosion thermonuclear bomb design. The former LST HMS *Narvik*, acting as the HQ and control ship for the tests, served as the platform for photographers from the Fleet Photographic Unit, who recorded this event unaware of the future implications of radiation exposure. The bomb pictured code-named 'Green Granite Small,' was dropped from a Valiant bomber of 49 Squadron RAF, producing a yield of 200–300 kilotonnes on detonation.

was prepared at Lossiemouth. The Peregrine Trophy award was instituted during this period by Alec J. Sturgenor, a former RN photographer and at the time editor of *Practical Photographer* magazine. Instituted to perpetuate the memory of the old school at RNAS Ford, the Trophy was intended to provide an annual focal point for the year's efforts and facilitate branch cohesion with an annual reunion every year. Mr Sturgenor also helped the Branch with public relations, publishing a major article about it in 1961. The opening paragraph set the tone of the article:

> 'Set in the heart of the Sussex countryside, approached through miles of semi-deserted lanes, is a disused airfield, once a hive of furious activity, and belonging to the Fleet Air Arm. Drive through the main gate and you find a school of photography with standards as high as any similar establishment in the world. Operated by the Royal Navy, it is used to train would-be photographers for the Navy, for the Army, and for the Royal Marines'.

The magazine also detailed some of the equipment in use in the early 1960s, including the Reid 35mm camera, Rolleicord VA, the Peckham Wray press camera and the De Vere monorail kits which were still in use at RAF Cosford in the late 1980s. Amazingly, candidates for the Branch were required to take IQ tests and see a psychologist, who decided whether they were suitable for the specialisation. It is indeed fortunate that these formalities were dispensed with by the 1980s, as the Branch would otherwise be considerably smaller than it is at present.

In 1963 the RN School of Photography duly moved to HMS *Fulmar*, Lossiemouth, under the command of Lt-Cdr 'Barney' Barron RN. At this large air station the Air Reconnaissance School was co-located with the school, possessing a Hawker Hunter GA11 and a photo-reconnaissance pilot for training purposes. 764 Hunter Squadron was on the other side of the airfield from the section, so the section was also given a scooter and sidecar to expedite the processing of recce film. Marked with the initials of the unit on the chimney ('P & ARS'), the combined school was nicknamed 'The Soap Factory'.

Lt-Cdr Barron caused his staff and trainees some concern in 1963 whilst flying a black-painted Sea Hawk jet on trials involving filmed maps in the cockpit. During the sortie he experienced engine failure and therefore ejected, depositing the aircraft in a Scottish loch. After his parachute landing, he promptly retired to the local pub for a few necessary drinks before telephoning the Naval Air Station to report in. Those waiting for news on the steps of the school were greatly relieved to hear he was safe.

At the RNSOP, CPO(Phot) Ray Bromelow became chief instructor, responsible for syllabus formation and teaching until his retirement in 1965, which event marked the end of a tradition, as he was the last serving person to wear the old style 'camera' badge. In 1965, the school requalified its exemption from examination by the Institute of Incorporated Photographers – a significant civilian recognition of the high degree of professionalism achieved. There were around two hundred and fifty ratings in the Branch at this time, including some very able candidates undergoing Special Duties (Aviation) officer training *en route* to achieving a commission. Several of these ratings returned to the Photographic Branch after obligatory out-of-trade time, a sensible policy that ensured good leadership at the highest echelons of the Branch with the degree of knowledge needed for a deeply specialist branch.

Branch newsletters for these years are valuable records of the diversity of units and sections that were available for drafts. In addition to attachments to the major surface units HMS *Eagle*, *Albion*, *Hermes*, *Bulwark*, *Intrepid*. *Fearless*, *Endurance*, *Britannia*, *Ark Royal* and *Victorious*, there were five ratings attached to Naval Air Squadrons plus large sections at Naval Air Stations and naval shore establishments. Some sections could actually field football teams; an idea almost incomprehensible to those who have followed in their footsteps.

In the section on 6E deck of HMS *Hermes*, the seven-man section prepared ship for sea in 1966. They returned the F46 Swordfish torpedo recording cameras sent through Naval Stores with typical understatement as 'no longer required'. Flying trials on board were filmed using a special bracket welded to the centre of the rounddown, photographing undercarriage response on aircraft landings. A particular memorable incident

Above:
Escorted by Admiral Evans (FOCAS) and Captain J.B. Frewen RN, HRH Prince Charles and HM the Queen visited HMS *Eagle* on Wednesday 29 April 1959 in Weymouth Bay. Using his own distinctive 5 x 4 Speed Graphic camera, LA(Phot) Rod Safe took a photograph of this charming group.

Above right:
PHOTEX (photographic exercise) sorties in rough weather can produce some of the most dramatic pictures of warships in their element. The 'Co' class HMS *Contest* was the first all-welded construction destroyer to enter service in the Royal Navy, joining the Sixth Destroyer Squadron after being fitted for minelaying. She is seen here ploughing through heavy seas on 10 April 1958.

Right:
This picture of HMS *Victorious*, carrying a full complement of Scimitars, Venoms and Skyraiders, was taken by LA(Phot) Tony Fisher in the Mediterranean during autumn 1959. It was reproduced with the caption, 'Photographers are encouraged to take pictures which have a dramatic angle as distinct from a technical aspect. Back lighting has been used for this impact full shot showing the venomous sting packed by a modern aircraft carrier. There is plenty of scope for any photographer having an artistic temperament and a desire to take other than record pictures'. LA(Phot) Paul Yockney served on the carrier as the 803 Squadron's photographer, operating Scimitars. A requirement was identified for a pilot's-eye view of the carrier to be taken by the forward-facing camera in the nose of a Scimitar. However, the camera would be unable to function due to interlocks if the undercarriage was down. Despite heavy losses of the Scimitar from carriers at sea, one of the squadron pilots seriously volunteered to fly with a screwdriver jammed in the interlock mechanism! The sortie was fortunately cancelled.

occurred when a morning's work was lost; the arrester hook of a Gannet AEW aircraft knocked the top off the HS300 camera magazine, allowing the exposed film to spew out all over the deck.

Also recorded in the newsletters are apocryphal stories from this period, referring to the behaviour of certain individuals within the Branch. It is probably wisest to draw a veil of charity over them, but it can safely be said that traditional Photographic Branch pastimes such as excessive consumption of alcohol, sale of large numbers of photographs and the pursuit of the 'fairer' sex featured heavily. One rating was reputed to have pawned the section equipment when he ran out of money, whilst another received an excessively large delivery of film from Naval Stores and sold the excess before Stores demanded it to be returned. Regrettably, there is only anecdotal evidence to support the story that a certain Chief Petty Officer had refused to leave a torpedoed carrier in the Mediterranean during the War without the 'rabbit' firm money, but it is a nice contemporary story. The station photographer at RNAS Abbotsinch was particularly fortunate – his section was next to the WRNS accommodation, with no intervening fence.

However, it may be fairly said that this period was one of the highlights in the various fortunes of the Branch – well manned, with good equipment and a cohesive and disciplined approach to a clearly defined task. There was also still a career structure, with sensible demographic manipulation to allow progression to higher rates and indeed, ranks. Director-General (Aircraft) was the directorate charged with the supply of equipment and materials, staffed by experienced former rating photographers who were aware of the fleet's needs.

Left:
Indicative of the problems experienced with the Scimitar at sea, these two shots depict the ejection of Lt J. Purvis from cab 154 of 803 Naval Air Squadron in November 1960. Captured by the Duty Photographer on top of Flying Control (FlyCo), the aircraft experienced centre of gravity and associated trim problems after launch from HMS *Victorious* in the Mediterranean, and was abandoned at the last moment by the pilot (who survived).

CAPE TIMES

FINAL

Established 1876 ★ TUESDAY, FEBRUARY 28, 1961 *(Registered at the G.P.O. as a Newspaper)* Price 2½c (3d.)

There was a stir on board HMS Victorious, the British aircraft-carrier visiting Cape Town, when models posed on the flight deck for a fashion photographer yesterday. Here Naval Airman Paul Yockeny takes one for the crew. The models are, left to right: Angela Ceronie, Trudy Prins, Barbro Klootwyk, a visiting Swedish model, and Elizabeth Woof. Report on this page.

Above:
HMS *Victorious* visited Cape Town at the end of February 1961, and permission was granted for a civilian photographer to photograph some international models on the flight deck. Unusually, one of the photographers on board was also recorded as he took shots with a Peckham Wray camera for the ship's public relations use, and the resulting image of LA(Phot) Paul Yockney appeared on the front page of the *Cape Times* on 28 February 1961.

Below:
The opportunities for photography in the RN of the 1950s were greatly enhanced by the impressive number of ships and aircraft in service. In November 1960, HMS *Victorious* leads HMS *Ark Royal* and HMS *Hermes* in the Mediterranean.

Right:
The mighty backdrop of the Forth Bridge sets off HMS *Hermes* on 5 September 1960, as she enters the Naval Base at Rosyth with Sea Vixen aircraft on deck.

Right below:
Record photography of special events such as flypasts and aerial work demands considerable experience. The results of this photography are shown in this shot of HMS *Ark Royal*, overflown by six Whirlwind HAS Mk 7s of 824 Naval Air Squadron during refuelling at sea with a 'Wave' class tanker on 15 September 1960.

Below:
A stunning high level shot of HMS *Victorious*, taken in 1961.

Below:
NA(Phot) Maurice 'Jan' Larcombe rose to senior positions in the Branch of the 1980s, eventually retiring as a Lieutenant-Commander. This period shot shows him with an F24 camera after completing a photographic tasking, flying in a Whirlwind helicopter during 1962.

The Royal Navy continued to conduct operations worldwide, in which the Branch occasionally played an important role. For example, in the early 1960s, Captain (later Admiral) Gibson of HMS *Ark Royal* escaped official censure when the carrier went aground in the Hamoaze at Plymouth. The ship's photographer, closed up as normal on the bridge for entering and leaving harbour, successfully recorded the incorrect positioning of the channel buoys, evidence which was successfully used for the defence. The on-the-spot availability of the Service photographer has always been the significant advantage over contract or civilian services, in addition to the clear benefits of in-house control and accountability.

Left:
Taken during the early 1960s, this image shows a Sea Vixen FAW1 on approach to HMS *Ark Royal*.

Left middle:
There has always been a small requirement for air-to-air pictures of some of the most photogenic hardware that the Navy possesses – its aircraft. NA(Phot) 'Jan' Larcombe photographed these four Buccaneers of 700B trials flight in formation on 20 May 1965, shooting with a Koni-Omega camera from a twin-seat Hunter. His logbook, kept as a mandatory requirement for entitlement to Flying Extra pay, records some flights that would turn present day photographers green with jealousy: Sea Vampire sorties to cine film coastlines, Buccaneer flights to photograph other Buccaneers, Sea Vixen formations over Hermes, Phantoms over HMS *Ark Royal* – the list goes on.

Above:
Renonnaissance was still an important role for the RN at Lossiemouth, so the phot section was regularly exercised in the loading of magazines, processing of film and rapid turn-around of material. A photo-story of the time records the process in full, depicting NA(Phot) Price as he changes the magazines in the nose of PR Hunter of 764 NAS on 30 June 1965. This clearly shows that photographers were allowed to 'sign for' (be responsible for) work on this aspect of aircraft, a sensible distinction that has not survived. On today's Sea Harrier aircraft, only specialist trade ratings are allowed to fit the F95 magazines, which are notoriously tricky. Over Bosnia with 800 NAS between 1993–5, this policy resulted in many lost recce films and almost caused the revision of this policy (back to the photographers fitting the magazines).

Left:
Photographed on trials under the Red Ensign in early 1963, HMS *Dreadnought* was commissioned in 1963 as Britain's first nuclear-propelled submarine. Assisting in building up the Royal Navy's core of experience in nuclear submarines, *Dreadnought* also achieved prominence when she became the first British submarine to surface at the North Pole in 1970.

PROGRESS

A beautiful air-to-air picture from this period, showing the most famous and (at the time) latest Fleet Air Arm jet aircraft together on 7 October 1966. HMS *Heron*'s Swordfish was briefed to form up with the Buccaneer from HMS *Eagle* over Glastonbury in Somerset, where PO(Phot) Paul Yockney recorded the formation from a Wasp helicopter, using an F24 camera with an 8-inch lens.

On 29 November 1967 British forces were withdrawn from Aden. Royal Marine patrols in the 'windmill' area inland of the colony were particularly pleased to be picked up by the 'old faithful' Wessex Mk 5 helicopter, and are seen here being evacuated from a ridge near Shaykh Uthman by an aircraft of 848 Naval Air Squadron, HMS *Albion*. Paul Yockney took this superb action shot on a Koni-Omega camera fitted with a 90mm lens. The decidedly hazardous circumstances are illustrated by the starboard 7.62mm general purpose machine-gun fitted to the helo.

A far-reaching event with ramifications for the whole Branch took place when the School of Photography at RAF Cosford was formally opened on 3 December 1965. The slowly-contracting Services had begun to realise the apparent benefits of centralisation to train photographers, setting up a Joint Service Training Group to examine the way ahead. However, policy makers within the Branch resisted the proposals, arguing that Tri-Service training did not allow the firm command and control that such a small specialist Royal Navy branch required. Unfortunately, the rate of change within the Armed Services was slow but inexorable, as future events were to prove, although it is fair to say with hindsight that many of these fears were well grounded.

Moves into new technology were heralded in February 1968 when the brand new CCTV studio opened at Jervis Block, HMS *Nelson*, giving the facility to instantly playback interviews and other footage – a faculty often used to train Senior Officers to deal with media attentions. The HS 300 high-speed cine camera was in serious use at the Fleet Photographic Unit (FPU), based at Fraser Barracks, Eastney. It was used to cover Phantom landings on board HMS *Eagle*, Wessex Mk 3 helicopter and Harrier trials on board HMS *Blake* and Sea King landing limits on board *Engadine*, and required the processing of 25,000 feet of film every month. The FPU moved to new buildings two years later, where it was soon to be joined by the co-located Royal Navy School of Applied Photography (RNSAP).

Photographer's luck continued at sea in 1967, when Naval Airman (Phot) Chadwick survived the ditching of a helicopter on board HMS *Hermes* during wind speed trials. Occupying the co-pilot's seat of the 'plane guard' safety helicopter, which had lowered a bomb-shaped weight as part of the exercise, he was airborne when a Sea Vixen ditched immediately after take-off. The Search and Rescue helicopter closed to rescue the aircrew who had ejected, but was itself struck by the ship and knocked into the sea. Having just completed underwater escape drills before sailing, Chadwick remembered his training and was fortunate enough to escape from the inverted aircraft.

The film-making side of the Branch was successful too, with PO(Phot) Gentry producing several films that were shown on UK television. HMS *Eagle*'s section further distinguished itself by covering the end of Sir Francis Chichester's round the world trip; NA(Phot) Geoff Sellars's pictures occupied half sheets in newspapers the following day. The *Blue Peter* presenter John Noakes' visit to the carrier was broadcast on national television that autumn featuring more aerials filmed by Geoff Sellars. Most of the work was still done in monochrome, so it is interesting to see that HMS *Osprey* (Portland) manufactured a display for the Paris Air Show, showing the mighty Wasp helicopter and 'including colour prints'. A perennial tasking for HMS *Osprey* was the regular Distex disaster simulations for ships working up at Portland, where a ruined town was simulated and disaster relief required. Photographers were sent to simulate press attention and, posing as journalists, questioned Commanding Officers about events. Different ships had different ideas about the press and how to treat them, so some phots came back merry, some received coffee only and some were arrested and thrown in cells. The Fleet Photographic Unit in Singapore (HMS *Simbang*) was also busy, plotting results from the conducted trial Firefish torpedo firings.

HMS *Albion* was off Aden during the build-up and actual withdrawal of British forces, with the two rival factions ashore (NLF and FLOSSY) fighting for control. Both were inclined to regard the Wessex Mk 5 helicopters as legitimate targets, so photographers '. . . took to lying flat on the floor with the ever faithful F24 between me and the outside world'. Having seen the photographic material depicting counter-insurgency events ashore, no chances were taken.

In 1969, it was deemed necessary to recruit and employ a limited number of Wren Photographic Assistants to alleviate the work burden and the manpower shortage, with only 160 ratings in the Branch. Seven ladies were trained at Lossiemouth and drafted accordingly, clearly doing the excellent job that Wrens have always done in the Branch, as June 1972 saw the introduction of a permanent WRNS branch. A twelve-week basic instruction course was introduced for Wren photographers, ten weeks for Leading Wren photographers and six weeks for POWren Phots. Serving only in shore bases, these women complemented the male ratings throughout the Navy becoming a great asset as they rose through the hierarchy, some ascending to Commissioned Rank. Lt-Cdr Jane Grimley (née Burridge), who rose to command the specialisation, and Lt Jan Green were highly regarded by the 'troops' for their efforts to preserve the Branch as matters grew worse in later days. Chief Petty Officer WRNS, particularly 'Jan' Redfearn and Kath Thomas, also made their mark, doing a superb job in running sections whilst remaining very popular with those who served under them.

To the consternation of many old hands, RNAS Lossiemouth eventually closed as an RN Air Station, handed over to the RAF on 29 September 1972. The RN School of Photography, now renamed the RN School of Applied Photography (RNSAP) for political reasons, therefore moved to the Fraser building in HMS *Excellent*, co-located with the existing section after the decision was taken to make basic training a Tri-Service venture. This co-location only lasted for a brief period, as the task of the first Senior Instructor, Sub-Lt M. 'Jan' Larcombe RN, was to design, build and equip the new

Above:
Routine flying operations on board HMS *Albion* off Singapore in the late 1960s allowed experimentation, seen here in the form of a time-exposure of 848 NAS Wessex Mk 5 helicopters during night operations. It was taken on 5″ x 4″ film format with an MPP large-format camera from the top of FlyCo.

Left:
This picture, regarded by many as one of the best shots of HMS *Ark Royal*, was taken by Lt 'Jan' Larcombe in 1970 with a Koni-Omega camera. The carrier has Phantom FG1s of 892 NAS and Buccaneer S2s of 809 NAS embarked on board.

Above:
An atmospheric shot of HMS *Albion* at 0700 hours in the Jahore Strait off Singapore on 22 May 1971 – taken with a Koni-Omega camera by LA(Phot) McKnight.

Right:
A nice example of the 'end of cruise' print routinely produced for 'rabbit' sale at the end of each trip. The map would be obtained from the navigation section, rephotographed and printed to 15″ x 12″ and then decorated with pictures and places relevant to the trip before reduction to 10″ x 8″. This example shows HMS *Albion*'s 'cruise chart' for 1971, sailing on the 26 March of that year and returning to Portsmouth at the end of January 1972.

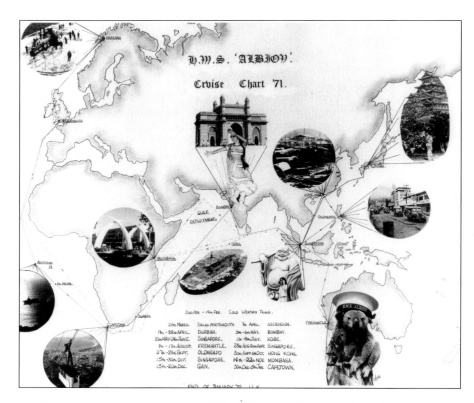

Below:
Service public relations has moved with the times, especially from the 1970s when in common with dreadful clothes and sideburns for men, women were photographed as a novelty on ships and displayed prominently on the cover of *Navy News*. These models look happy as they pose in Malta with a Phantom in 1974.

Below:
On 21 September 1977 HRH the Prince of Wales visited HMS *Ark Royal*, taking the opportunity to fly in the back seat for a steam catapult launch in a Buccaneer. Photographed on deck, he was presented with a shot of his launch immediately after his flight.

building at the wardroom end of West Battery. Training for advanced career courses (Phot 1s) and WRNS remained at the RNSAP, where the staff hoped to install a naval ethos into senior trainees. The RNSAP changed designation again later, to the RN School of Advanced Photography, a title that more properly reflected its role at the time. However, the Joint School of Photography (JSOP) at RAF Cosford, built in 1965 as the largest purpose-built photographic school in Europe, became the first experience of photography for a new generation of Royal Navy ratings.

At DGA(N), responsible for the introduction of equipment to the Branch, the experienced team under Lt-Cdr Paul Johnson RN recognised the need for a new camera system in late 1972 / early 1973. A search amongst the industry was therefore commenced, which resulted in the procurement of the superb medium-format 120 Hasselblad camera for the Royal Navy. When the system was first demonstrated to DGA(N) by Hasselblad (UK) representatives, the initial reaction was quite simply that it was too expensive. However, mindful of previous experiences with bad cameras and recognising the Hasselblad's sheer quality, the huge primary outlay was spread over in a ten-year budget plan. This wise decision has been repeatedly vindicated, particularly as the very same cameras are still in service twenty-five years later. A new enlarger type, the De Vere 504, was also purchased in bulk and distributed to sections, and the growing field of 35mm was not ignored, represented by the acquisition of the Nikon F2. Finally, the department concerned itself with the design of the 'Invincible' class photographic departments, ensuring relocation to 2 Deck where the 'air world' congregate on a carrier.

Farsightedly, drawing on the pool of specialist experience at the department, 'Kodak' Versamat through-bulkhead processors were acquired and fitted to process reconnaissance film at very high speeds, allowing speedy analysis. These procurement decisions have had far-reaching repercussions for the Branch in the 1980s and 1990s, facilitating high quality work in shore bases and sections in which to serve out the few sea drafts still available.

Whilst these important developments took place on the procurement front, normal section work and training took place, maintaining phot services to the rest of the Royal Navy, and concentrated on preserving a career structure within the Branch. As the whole Navy began to constrict, reflecting the increasing move towards accountability, budgeting and rationalisation, the first of increasingly aggressive truncation proposals for the specialisation was proposed. Intially, a cohesive response by the Head of the Branch, usually after a meeting of all the Photographic Officers available, effectively dealt with the threats.

Above:
It has been the photographer's lot since the 1930s to stand on deck and film/video the launch and recovery of aircraft. LA(Phot) Steve Pratt prepares to record the launch of a Phantom aircraft from HMS *Ark Royal*.

Left:
The raw power of conventional fixed wing aircraft is an experience lost to the Royal Navy that approaches the millennium. An unforgettable experience to photographers, it is interesting to remember that phot ratings proceeding through the commissioning process often served time as Flight Deck Officers (FDO 3/4). A Phantom launches from HMS *Ark Royal* in the mid-1970s.

On the front line during 1976, photographers from the Fleet Photographic Unit were sent on *roulement* from HMS *Excellent* to photograph the 'Cod War' fishing dispute in the Iceland/Faeroes gap. Working under the dreadful weather conditions routinely experienced in this area, several graphic images of the confrontation were obtained which featured heavily in the world's press.

The spirit of rationalisation now endemic in the Armed Forces continued to demand change, manifested once again in the closure of the traditional home of the Gunnery Branch, HMS *Excellent*, in 1985. This naturally caused the Gunnery School considerable upset, as the dead hand of tradition rests heavily on the Royal Navy in general, but the photographic section moved back to the old Tipner site, where everything had begun over sixty years ago. Concerns about attachment to HMS *Excellent*, particularly as a 'tail' unit vulnerable to cuts, led to a successful attempt by senior Branch officers to have the unit transferred to the line authority of Commander-in-Chief Fleet at Northwood, an action that certainly staved off manpower reductions. Record sheets for this period indicate the result of decreased recruiting, which combined with natural wastage had reduced numbers to 150 ratings, which included 40 Wren photographers.

Above:
Photographers were deployed to the unpleasant series of fishery incidents that became collectively known as the 'Cod Wars'. The pictures taken were widely published at the time, especially this shot taken on HMS *Juno* on 7 February 1976. It depicts the actual moment that the Icelandic gunboat *Baldur* made a run in, attempting to cut the nets of the British Trawler *Kingston Beryl*.

Left:
Some photographers through experience became very adept at weapons recording, calibration and trials, and good colour pictures of expensive weaponry are always useful for recruiting material. A Guided Missile Destroyer (GMD) of the late 1970s fires the gigantic Sea Slug missile, which was encased in solid fuel booster rockets to accelerate the beast to operating velocity. The Sea Slug was famous for what was colloquially known as the 'f**k me' response shown by crowds of observers in close proximity, who as a group could be observed involuntarily bending back from the waist up as the 22-foot long missile ignited and blasted off.

THE FALKLANDS CONFLICT

Above:
Always technically inferior to posed shots, the real action picture nevertheless has an immediacy and realism all of its own. The frigate HMS *Plymouth* provides Naval Gunfire Support (NGS) inland with its twin 4.5-inch Mk 6 guns during Operation *Paraquat*, the retaking of South Georgia on 25 April 1982.

Above:
No contract photography will ever satisfactorily replace the RN photographer at sea. On-the-spot access, competence and experience in naval ways are demonstrated in this shot, the actual moment the surrender of South Georgia was signed by the Argentinian Captain Alfredo Astiz in the wardroom of HMS *Plymouth*. LA(Phot) Nigel 'Darbi' Allen recorded this scene on 20 April 1982, which was witnessed by Captain Young RN of HMS *Antrim*, Captain Nick Barber RN of HMS *Endurance* and Major Guy Sheridan RM.

I n common with the entire world, the Royal Navy was caught unawares by the sudden flare-up of the Falklands Conflict, which many believed was concerned with a group of islands somewhere off Scotland. Responding to the situation, the truly British spirit of overcoming the impossible was demonstrated throughout the Service – nicely reflected in RNAS Culdrose photographic section's contribution to the emergency. Recognition material was urgently required by the fleet travelling south, because little material on the Argentinian military was available for Command briefings. LA(Phot) Brian Jones was working over Easter leave in 1982 when the urgent requirement for Argentinian aircraft pictures was passed to the section. After recalling LA(Phot) 'Bernie' Pettersen, the two photographers obtained models of the Super Etendard, Mirage, Pucará and other Argentinian aircraft from the recognition cell. Echoing the work of the Aircraft Recognition Cell during the Second World War, a black backdrop was arranged in the section while the aircraft were suspended from pieces of thread. Eight-point views of each plane followed – the results of which were printed forty times onto 12″ × 10″ ortho film and dispatched as viewgraphs to each ship in the Task Force.

Rather more prepared were the photographers attached to the Commando Forces News Team, who were kept busy before departure reproducing intelligence material relating to the potential invasion, notably the coastline views collected by Colonel Ewan Southby-Tailyour RM on his now-famous sailing expedition around the Islands. PO(Phot)s Alastair Campbell and Roger Ryan sailed for the Islands in the SS *Canberra*, whilst PO(Phot) Pete Holdgate and Sgt. Dave Munnelly of the Commando Forces News Team departed on board HMS *Fearless*. After consolidating the massive build-up of forces on Ascension Island, the Task Force sailed south as diplomatic efforts failed to resolve the deadlock.

Whilst off Ascension Island, the military planning continued, exploring several options until the decision was taken to force a bridgehead in San Carlos Water. Captain Dave Nichols RM, leading the Commando Forces News Team, deployed with his team who were allowed complete autonomy in their task once ashore – an enlightened decision that allowed them to accompany various units of the Royal Marines as they 'yomped' across the campaign field. With 35mm camera equipment jammed into two old respirator bags, and armed with an Armalite rifle and 9mm pistol, PO(Phot) Holdgate transferred with 40 Commando RM to landing craft just after midnight on 21 May. They then held off the beach until Naval Gunfire Support and Special Forces had neutralised an Argentinian observation point on Fanning Head. Landing on Blue Beach at 0430 hours, the Royal Marines dug in for the expected air attacks and patrolled the area while larger contingents of men and supplies were landed. The News Team had previously borrowed a very large Union Jack Battle Ensign from HMS *Fearless*, and took this opportunity to run up the first British flag on the Islands for press photographs, in the settlement manager's garden at San Carlos. The flag itself was taken down only two hours later because another Argentinian observation post overlooked the site, but this historic photograph was transmitted (by Martin Cleaver of the Press Association) straight to London, and was personally shown in the House of Commons by the Prime Minister, Margaret Thatcher.

The expected air attacks materialised shortly after the beach-head was established, turning San Carlos Water into 'Bomb Alley' as the Argentinian

Left:
The day before the landing to retake the Falkland Islands, the decision was taken to disperse the raiding force in case of air attack. Accordingly, landing craft were used on 20 May to cross-deck Royal Marines from 40 Cdo from *Canberra* to HMS *Fearless*, producing an opportunity for 'Al' Campbell's Hasselblad camera.

Air Force passed home its attacks with great bravery against the mass of shipping in the narrow inlet. The attacks would regularly come in at around 10a.m. and 2p.m., so PO(Phot) Holdgate would go out onto the end of the small jetty with his Nikon F2 and 135mm lens, recording the low-level jets as they attacked the ships. (Well known photographs from this time include the Mirage fighter seen between the masts of HMS *Fearless*, the bombing of HMS *Plymouth* and the sinking of HMS *Antelope*.) However, the Argentinians had spotted the concentration of activity around the dug-in Headquarters at San Carlos and called in an air attack from north to south, which duly arrived while he was on the jetty. He recalls, 'It was coming straight for me, so low that I could clearly see up the intakes (of the Skyhawk) and the pilot's face. I could hear people calling my name behind me, but everything went into slow motion as the two bombs came off the aircraft'. Two parachute-retarded bombs landed in the water at the landward end of the jetty, about 30 metres away from the photographer, who watched in amazement as the parachutes settled in the water. Fortunately, the aircraft had been so low that the impeller fuses on the bombs were not wound in sufficiently to 'arm' the bombs, which were later destroyed in controlled explosions.

After the initial landings PO(Phot) Holdgate and Sgt Dave Munnelly detached to cover some of the other newsworthy events of the conflict on land, including the aftermath of the Battle for Goose Green, when the prisoners were led away with the gorse still on fire. After photographing the burials of the dead, the team travelled to Teal Inlet and on to Mount Kent with 42 Cdo RM, accompanying LA(Phot) Roger Ryan who was attached to the unit. The briefing for the assault on Mount Harriet followed, which began at 0030 hours on 12 June. Pete Holdgate remembers the sheer volume of fire from the defenders, especially the tracer, because for every round seen burning there were at least another four bullets in the air unseen.

Moving to join 45 Cdo RM, who had launched a simultaneous attack on Two Sisters, the News Team finally marched into Port Stanley, 'liberating' a Falklands Islands flag from an Argentinian prisoner *en route*. Rounding up the members of Juliet Company RM, the unit which had originally been forced to surrender during the invasion as Naval Party 8901, photographs of the now-victorious unit were taken with the Island's flag. The defeated army was disarmed at Stanley Airfield and pictures were taken of the prisoners, who called out 'Bobby Charlton' and 'Jimmy Greaves' to the photographers as they worked.

In retrospect, those who were fortunate enough to go ashore produced the most memorable images of the conflict, particularly the professionals attached to the Royal Marine units, who accompanied them throughout.

Director Public Relations (Navy) (DPR(N)) photographic staff had less opportunity to go ashore, whilst the operational requirement to keep the high-value carrier assets away from air attack meant that photographic

Below:
Marching from Two Sisters to Port Stanley with men of 45 Cdo RM, walking in each other's footsteps because of the threat of mines, PO(Phot) Pete Holdgate spotted the opportunity for a picture of a Royal marine who had placed a flag on his radio aerial. Using the 50mm lens on his Nikon F2, he spontaneously took black and white negative and colour transparency pictures, without interrupting the column; this photograph came to symbolise the conflict for many and is now immortalised as a statue outside the Royal Marines Museum at Eastney Barracks, Portsmouth.

Right:
PO(Phot) 'Paddy' Ryan routinely
photographed the scene as 'J' Company of
42 Cdo Royal Marines prepared their
equipment in the old seaplane shed at Port
Stanley. It was not until the film was
processed by 'Al' Campbell back on the
Canberra, that the section realised he had
produced one of the most remarkable Royal
Marines photographs ever taken.

Below:
The return of the victorious Task Force was
a cause for national rejoicing. On 21 July
1982 HMS *Hermes*, bearing the scars of her
battering by the South Atlantic, returns to
Portsmouth Harbour, welcomed by a flotilla
of small ships and the photographers of the
Fleet Photographic Unit.

sections on HMS *Hermes* and HMS *Invincible* only saw the conflict through the reconnaissance pictures they dealt with. Processed on board every day, this reconnaissance was carried out by Sea Harrier F95 cameras fitted with short focal-length lenses. The interpretation of these photographs was greatly hampered by the lack of RN Photo Interpretation (PI) officers in the Task Force. (This deficiency was again highlighted during Adriatic operations fourteen years later, when it became clear that the PI specialisation had degraded still further). LA(Phot) Rick Toyer was on board the landing ship HMS *Fearless* to record the first landing of a Sea Harrier, which was short of fuel after combat, and also recorded atmospheric shots of HMS *Plymouth* on fire in San Carlos Water. When the *Atlantic Conveyor* was sunk two photographers were on board, fortunately both escaped unscathed apart from the loss of all equipment.

At home, the Branch tested two reconnaissance pods for Lynx and Sea King helicopters, the Vicon and Vipa 2, which were acquired, tested and dispatched in six days. Neither was ever used in anger – the Vipa 2 was also never seen again, and is believed still in transit.

Due to the Exocet missile threat, HMS *Hermes* spent three months outside the Total Exclusion Zone, in which time the photographic section provided news for the Ship's Company, reconnaissance film processing and record coverage. The return of the Task Force from the Falklands was a great celebration, and naturally Ships' Companies were keen to acquire photographic records of the great undertaking that they had experienced. On board HMS *Hermes*, the section quickly ran out of the privately-purchased 'rabbit' paper, a worrying discovery as there was clearly a great market to be tapped. Fortunately, Captain Lyn Middleton RN was rightly persuaded that it was good public relations to meet the demand for pictures to the Ship's Company, so the section sold every sheet of paper on board before arrival in Portsmouth – a great achievement.

Even after purchasing all the paper to return to the MoD and after all this legitimate hard work, there must have been sufficient funds to give each section member 'photographer's back'; an unusual medical condition suffered by RN phots on ships through the ages as they lift heavy sacks of money. This dreadful affliction still 'curses' some of those unfortunate enough to serve on aircraft carriers today.

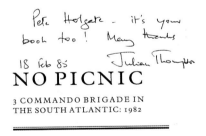

Pete Holgate – it's your book too! Many thanks

18 Feb 85 Julian Thompson

NO PICNIC

3 COMMANDO BRIGADE IN
THE SOUTH ATLANTIC: 1982

Julian Thompson

MARCH TO THE
SOUTH ATLANTIC

To Chief Petty Officer Pete Holgate. Whose photographs add so much to this account in which he played such an outstanding, operational role

Nick Vaux.
CO 42 Cdo RM 1982

Left:
The personal bravery of the Commando-trained Branch ratings in the Falklands Conflict demonstrated the advantages of the trained professional photographer in the field – PO(Phot) Pete Holdgate is pictured here on Mount Kent days before the 42 Royal Marine Commando night attack on Mount Harriet. Reproduced on the right are comments regarding PO(Phot) Holdgate's role from Major-General Julian Thompson RM and Nick Vaux, the Commanding Officer of 42 Commando RM during the conflict.

BRANCH ARCHIVES

I n the rush and urgency of the 1982 conflict, particularly with the intense media scrutiny that found the Navy unprepared for journalists, several fundamental organisational weaknesses were highlighted that still have severe repercussions. For example, when PO(Phot) Pete Holdgate handed over his original transparency films from the Falklands War, they were taken back to the UK, processed and *given out*! As a result, the Royal Navy today possesses very little of the material from the conflict and is in the ludicrous position of having to search around picture libraries and publishers for its own imagery – a situation that need never have arisen if the importance of the material had been assessed.

This cavalier approach to vital material regrettably becomes a more common theme as the history of the Branch nears the present. Indeed, the picture research for this publication has relied heavily on what material photographers have personally retained, as the official files are badly kept, uncatalogued and routinely weeded by individuals who would not recognise an important negative if it assaulted them. The problem of historical material has long been overlooked in the Branch, with the result that priceless material has undoubtedly been lost for ever. Whilst there is undoubtedly a case for selective weeding of the files by someone who can recognise and differentiate between rubbish and that of value, this logical step has never been taken. An interesting historical perspective is offered by Paul Yockney, who served twenty-four years in the Branch and had contact with the Navy's archives at Fraser Gunnery Range before they transferred to Tipner again:

'When, in January 1969, I first entered the windowless, tiny, crammed room known as the library, I found that the previous librarian, a very junior rating, had put negatives in the "For Disposal" tray that were, in my humble opinion, quite priceless. For example, HMS *Furious* operating aircraft in, I think, the 1930s, capital ships sunk in World War Two and other negatives that could never be replaced. I also found some of the best negatives I'd taken of the *Centaur* in 1963–5 earmarked for ditching . . . I was amazed at the cavalier attitude that prevailed throughout the Branch [towards the negative library]'.

Although this is nearly thirty years ago, the situation still prevails. An ex-service photographer would be absolutely ideal to look after what is, after all, a national asset, but in the meantime the material continues to decay – a situation in sharp contrast to the Royal Marines, who have retained all their records and negatives to this day.

It is also salutary to remember the fate of the Photographic Branch Museum, which exhibited interesting photographs, artefacts and cameras from the Branch's chequered history. When the unit moved from *Excellent* to the Tipner site, the group photographs and a few cameras were sent to RAF Cosford. The remainder was destroyed. Located at Tipner during the handover from civilians to the Branch was film footage from the Second World War, including original American and German propaganda productions and the 'Mulberry' Harbour construction reel shot by Martin Curtis and Gordon Dines. Sets of wartime *Jane's Fighting Ships* and related publications were also secured in the cells behind the unit. All of this material has now gone.

History has cause to thank those who stole some of the material, for they at least ensured that something survived.

Below:
A classic example of a good public relations shot, this re-enactment of a night rescue won the Peregrine Trophy for LA(Phot) Brian Jones in 1983. Photographed from a Sea King helicopter, the chemical container ship *Craig-Antlet* ran aground in bad weather, breaking her back shortly after the rescue of her crew by 819 Naval Air Squadron from HMS *Gannet*. The original negative is almost certainly lost.

OPERATIONAL TASKING – INTELLIGENCE

Historically, the Photographic Branch has always possessed an intelligence-gathering capability, specially placed and trained to produce military imagery as required for the task. However, in two particular fields the specialisation has made noteworthy and substantial contributions – maritime and internal security.

World events of the mid-1980s generated a new operational role for the Branch, when the rise of the Soviet Navy became a grave cause of concern; especially the northern fleet which posed a significant threat to Britain's allocated NATO role on the Norwegian flank. Exercises such as 'Summerex '85' outlined below were deliberately engineered to demonstrate that the Soviet Fleet was ready and able to counter NATO amphibious landings such as, in war, might be carried out by the Royal Marines component of the UK/Netherlands Landing Force. One of the main functions of intelligence in peacetime is that of a monitoring tool, which requires the evaluation of material for trends, warnings and future operational planning. To assist with this important policy determinator, specialist training and equipment has been formulated by the Branch specifically in order to take advantage of intelligence opportunities.

Regrettably, explicit details of this tasking remain classified under statutory legislation, but open 'public' sources report much of historical relevance when traced through the time period under consideration. In 1985, HMS *Newcastle* monitored the activities of a Russian Maritime Battle Group 80 miles south-west of the Lofoten Islands off Northern Norway, shadowing the 43,000-ton Russian aircraft-carrier *Kiev* during a large-scale Russian exercise nicknamed 'Summerex '85' by NATO HQ. While *Kiev* recovered her air group of 'Forger' V/STOL aircraft to the deck, landing difficulties caused one of the fighters to crash into the sea; the pilot ejecting shortly before impact. A rigid inflatable boat from HMS *Newcastle* offered assistance until a 'Helix' helicopter from the carrier recovered the pilot. The resulting superb aerial picture of HMS *Newcastle* with the *Kiev* and the Soviet helicopter, taken by a member of the Branch, made the front page of *The Times* on Tuesday 23 July 1985 under the headline 'How the Navy saved a Soviet pilot'.

THE TIMES WEDNESDAY FEBRUARY 27 1985

Spotting Russia's deep-sea dinosaur

Typhoon at sea: One of the first photographs of the world's largest submarine, Russia's Typhoon, which was released yesterday by the Royal Navy (Rodney Cowton writes). This 24,000-ton giant is nearly 200 yards long, more than three times as heavy as a British Polaris submarine, and at least 6,000 tons heavier than the planned Trident submarine which will carry the next generation of Britain's strategic nuclear deterrent.

There is believed to be only one operational Typhoon, although a second is expected to enter service shortly, and a third is at an advanced stage of construction. It is armed with 20 SS-N20 nuclear missiles, each with a range of 5,000 miles. This means that it will be able to operate in some of the most remote ocean areas, and still remain within range of strategic targets.

The first Typhoon is thought so far to have remained in northern waters in the vicinity of the Barents Sea, relatively close to its base in the Kola Peninsula, and it was in the Barents Sea that the photograph was taken recently.

Left:
Extraordinary confirmation of the Royal Navy Photographic Branch's intelligence role appeared in *The Times* of 27 February 1985, when the Royal Navy released 'one of the first photographs of the world's largest submarine, Russia's Typhoon'; at 26,000-tons the same displacement as HMS *Invincible* and armed with twenty SS-N20 nuclear missiles. Taken in early 1985 in the Barents Sea close to its base in the Kola Peninsula, this picture was a major intelligence coup for the West.
(News International Newspapers)

Below:
Northern Ireland has always been a conundrum, as successive units of the British Forces attempt to police the tragic sectarian divide. The Royal Marines always take their own photographers, who provide forensic services and record photography, such as this shot of a Royal Marine from Forkhill Barracks on patrol in South Armargh 'bandit country'. The clipping from the *An Phoblacht* newspaper details intelligence allegations against the security forces. The picture shows a naval photographer at work.

REPUBLICAN NEWS, Thursday, June 16th, 1989

Brit spy team admitted

HE BRITISH ARMY have admitted that two soldiers posed as a TV camera team while filming outside a polling station in Derry City on May 17th, the day of the local Government elections. They claimed that the film was of "general scenes of security force activity" but Sinn Féin councillor, Hugh Brady, has said that the soldiers were on an intelligence gathering operation, filming people entering and leaving the polling station.

Brady stated:

"The soldiers had been filming for some time outside the St Cecilia's School polling station in Creggan when they were challenged by Sinn Féin election workers. When they asked what they were doing they said they were an independent crew attached to Ulster Television but when further asked to produce press cards they ran off to the bottom of Bligh's Lane where they were driven off in two waiting Land Rovers.

INTELLIGENCE PURPOSES

Councillor Brady continued that the incident had more "serious undertones" than the suggestion that they were 'innocently' recording their tour of duty: "These soldiers were filming people coming in and out of the polling centre. The film was obviously designed for some intelligence gathering purposes and it was also an attempt to intimidate voters. The electoral officer must

tion of this incident at the forthcoming EC elections. I would also urge that the media must strongly protest at what can only be described as a serious abuse of their position by the British army."

The National Union of Journalists are also calling on the British army to explain the conduct of the soldiers. NUJ broadcasting officer, John Foster, said it was 'quite irresponsible and placed other camera crews, technicians and journalists in "great jeopardy."

Ulster Television were contacted by Brady about the incident and UTV wrote to the British army to ask for an explanation. After receiving the British army version, UTV's managing director, Jim Creagh said that the company "took great exception" to anyone trying to represent themselves as a member of UTV staff. UTV staff and management were due to meet on Monday, June 12th, to discuss the matter further.

Reports of an alleged incident surfaced in the *Daily Mail* during October 1987, which although unconfirmed by the Ministry of Defence (Navy), brought the intelligence issue to the attention of the world's media. According to the paper, two Lynx helicopters were being flown at low level over the Barents Sea indicating the obvious proximity of RN surface assets, when they were overflown by Russian Su-27 fighter aircraft using their afterburners in an aggressive manoeuvre designed to force the helicopters into the sea. Only the skill of the aircrew involved saved the helicopters, and this dangerous conduct resulted in an official protest from the Ministry of Defence to the Soviet Air Force Commander in Moscow.

Further details of these operations are confirmed by the Royal Navy's stalwart *Navy News* paper, which carried an article in January 1988 under the ironic headline 'Smokey and the Bandit'. Confirming the uninvited presence of HMS *Liverpool* in the Barents Sea, the piece also specifically mentions the use of air assets to photograph joint gunnery and missile firings by the Russian Northern Fleet and air units. Additionally the publication *Snaps* (Maritime Press) confirmed the employment of the Branch in Naval intelligence at this time, graphically illustrated by the inclusion of an aerial photograph showing a Soviet Navy crew on the fin (conning tower) of their submarine – the marked photographic 'compression' effect experienced at extreme optical focal lengths clearly evident in the picture.

Finally, in 1996 the Russians alleged that the Royal Navy were again spying on defence bases and ships in the Arctic, using the Type-22 frigate HMS *London* and the Royal Fleet Auxiliary *Fort Grange* support vessel together with several submarines. Accused by an official Russian ITAR-TASS news agency of 'spying on Naval facilities in Northern Russia; and patrolling the Barents Sea', the Royal Navy insisted that 'we were going about our lawful business in international waters', insisting further that the units were keeping rigidly outside Russia's twelve-mile coastal limit. These operations have always been necessarily surrounded by a screen of security. It is, however, a matter of open record that the 1985/86/87 White Papers on Defence were unusually specific and accurate in their assessments of the Russian Northern Fleet. The litigation risk under Section 1(3) of the Official Secrets Act 1989 stifles open public record of the significant risks taken by the aircrew and photographers on these operations. It must therefore be left to the discretion of the reader, who may be aware of the level of access that the author has enjoyed after completing two such operations, to understand that much valuable and dangerous work has been done in this field with exceptional results.

Maritime intelligence is not the only area in which the Branch has undertaken extremely hazardous work with a higher degree of dedication and personal bravery. When Royal Marine units are posted to Northern Ireland, they are invariably accompanied by their photographer, who records their tour of duty and requirements as they arise. Obviously another sensitive area which cannot be safely outlined, these drafts demand specialist photographic training and are considered to produce material of great value to the security services.

For more than forty years, the main focus of British security and defence policy has been the threat to Western Europe posed by an ideologically hostile and massively-overarmed Soviet Union. The problem was highlighted by the amazing statistic that the USSR was allegedly producing a new submarine every six weeks in the late 1980s. Current operations and targets are obviously classified today, especially since the collapse of Soviet hegemony in Eastern Europe, the lifting of the Iron Curtain and the transformation of the intelligence task around the world. However, Military Task 1.11 in the United Kingdom Statements of Defence Estimates states 'Military intelligence is essential to any commander, and the Task encompasses the ability to collect intelligence by land, sea and air assets' . . . 'the Armed Forces assist GCHQ and other agencies in obtaining intelligence'. The Photographic Branch has made an important contribution to this field in the areas outlined above; a contribution which may never be fully revealed but has been pivotal over the years.

In April 1998, the Foreign Secretary Robin Cook paid an unprecedented tribute to the work of GCHQ and other UK intelligence agencies, stating; 'the results of their work cannot speak for themselves . . . the nature of what they do means that we cannot shout about their achievements if we want them to remain effective'. These words apply equally to the tasks undertaken by the Branch, and indicate a vital operational role for the Branch to play in the Royal Navy of the future.

UP TO
DATE

Until 1976, Naval Airman ratings for the Branch were selected as numbers permitted from the brightest trainees on the basic course. However, the reduced numbers required led to the decision to make the Branch 'sideways entry'; awarding the rate of acting Leading Rate on completion of the professional course. This meant that any rating who had aspirations to become a photographer now had to join the Royal Navy in another specialisation and pass for Leading Hand before having his papers sent to Flag Officer Naval Air Command (FONAC – the controlling authority) for selection as demographic criteria allowed. This convoluted process was further hampered by a severe lack of available information, unless ratings were fortunate enough to discover their local section and become 'phot groupies'.

Recommendation for release to the Branch by Commanding Officers was required in all cases, in a echo of the historical precedent of 1919 that stated 'Apply to Commanding Officers'. Many General Service Commanding Officers were not enthusiastic about ratings transferring to the Fleet Air Arm, perceived as a downwards move, and therefore success at this stage also relied on persuasive ability. A three-day acquaint in the section at HMS *Heron*, RNAS Yeovilton, followed during which the candidate gained a wider experience of the task and was examined regarding motivation and basic ability. This selection method certainly deterred the casual applicant, but left much to be desired in many areas, particularly as inadequate monitoring at HMS *Heron* could easily allow sub-standard material to reach the next stage – training at JSOP. It may also be pointed out that the new ratings entering the Branch were under no illusions about 'rabbit' work and its scope for exploitation, setting about this onerous task with a vengeance. The legacy left by the most efficient predators is still manifest in the General Service opinion of the Branch as a whole.

The Joint School of Photography is situated by the parade ground at RAF Cosford, near Albrighton and Wolverhampton. Staffed by Tri-Service instructors and backed by an impressively experienced civilian team (often ex-service), the school turned out a high number of trainees for the RN in the late 1980s and early 1990s. Mostly integrating well with the RAF, apart from some outrageous incidents, the Royal Navy course was intensive but popular, taking about seven months to complete with a main leave break. The proximity of the Cavalier and Oakleaf clubs and the hundreds of trainee WAAF telegraphists caused some distractions, although the RN failure rate was very low. The four-phase course comprised basic instruction in maths and optics, the dreaded Phase Two technical with the unforgettable Mr Hacon and CPO(Phot) Mick Cunningham, public relations (PR) and final exams in Phase Three; colour photography being introduced in Phase Four. Phase Two was particularly testing, involving the essential skills of technical photography and 760 (aircraft defect work), as well as architectural interiors and exteriors. The architectural subject often turned out to be the medieval Tong Church close to the camp, complete with its beautiful tombs and effigies. On many hot summers, trainees could not struggle any further on foot than the church, carrying the large monorail cameras and tripods essential to acquire the skills of non-diverging verticals in exterior building photography. The instructors and examination panels naturally saw more views of Tong Church than they cared for, and it became known as FTC for reasons that have since been lost in the mists of time. Most of the houses photographed were nicely framed with the leaves of a tree overhanging into the composition – invariably

Above:
The mural on the front wall of JSOP, familiar to every naval photographer since training, became Tri-Service in 1972. PO(Phot) Kev Preece, known as 'instructor boy' after his professional manner on the Petty Officer's Qualifying Course in 1992, kindly put aside his personal embarrassment to take this picture in 1997.

Right:
'Outback 1988' was another exercise for the Royal Navy to practise out-of-area capabilities. HMS *Illustrious* lies in Sydney Harbour whilst fireworks illuminates the Antipodean sky. (*PO(Phot) Ken Rixon*)

produced by another member of course holding a broken-off branch out of the field of view.

The course educated photographers to a very high standard, both practically and theoretically, and was recognised by the exemption of trainees from the exam of Licenciateship of the British Institute of Professional Photography on completion of the course and a short probationary period.

Concurrent with basic training ran the Phot 1s or Petty Officer's Qualifying Courses, so basic trainees often met the famous, infamous and downright notorious from the fleet for the first time in the coffee room at Stand-Easy. The standard of these Petty Officer's Qualifying Courses was also recognised by the British Institute of Professional Photographers, which awarded Associateship in HM Forces Photography on completion. A landmark event at JSOP in 1988 was the successful completion of the course by the first two sideways-entry Wren photographers, Leading Wrens Hepple and Keylock.

The long suffering naval hierarchy at JSOP policed the RN contingents and consequently spent much time inventing even more implausible excuses for some alarming incidents of Tri-Service communication breakdown. Of all the stories from this time, perhaps it is fortunate that the RAF never discovered the forty pints of home-brew that LA(Phot) 'Iggy' Smith brewed in a locker when living in Fulton block. Capable of inducing near-blindness, this special lager was bottled in a bath one weekend and tested on unsuspecting RAF trainees, who invariably left for Tibet the next morning wearing sunglasses.

The Photographic Branch has always had a normal cross-section of good, mediocre and bad photographers, the same as any other representative organisation, but in the middle to late eighties, hand-in-hand with advanced developments in camera and film technology, some individual photographers began to stand out for the excellence of their work. Possessing a good eye for a picture and driven by the urge for originality and quality so well inculcated at JSOP, Chris North, 'Fez' Parker, Alastair Campbell, Jon Garthwaite and a host of others took pictures which greatly impressed those under training at the time and acted as a spur to achieve. In particular, an astonishing 1987 photograph by Chris North gained worldwide acclaim and was widely disseminated to promote Royal Navy interests. Depicting a Lynx helicoper in rough weather hovering head-on in front of HMS *Minerva*, the image demonstrated that the photographer had used his considerable air-to-air experience to request the unusual aeronautical principle of 'cross control' from the pilots – manipulation of the aircraft controls to achieve a particular flight position and configuration.

At the end of 1987 the Branch had declined slightly in numbers, down to 127 personnel, and it is arguable that an unfortunate demographic decision was made, blocking the promotion rosters for years and causing frustrated ratings to leave the Service. Every year in the RN, 2OE (Second Open Engagement) boards sit to decide whether branches will be able to meet their tasks with the people they have, or if they should retain Senior Ratings by offering further 10-year engagements past the normal 22-year career break point. The purpose of this in large branches is to retain experienced personnel and in the main it is a successful tool for bridging manning gaps. However, promotion in a small branch is effectively governed by 'dead man's shoes', and as most of those serving are extremely healthy it is necessary to maintain the flow of people out of the Service, primarily to allow promotion of new deserving candidates. Instead of recognising this obvious management fact, the board chose to retain a number of senior Chief Petty Officers, thus artificially blocking the promotion roster unless someone literally died. This decision caused great upset in the Branch, as points levels to Petty Officer rose above one thousand – the highest in the Navy. To put this points figure in perspective, a rating on average points (seventy every six months) would wait a year after the basic course before taking the professional qualifying examination, two years before eligibility to accumulate points, followed by a further seven-and-a-half years for promotion.

A well-known Branch rating was provoked into writing an anonymous letter to *Navy News* requesting an explanation of the situation in May 1989. Entitled 'One Thousand and One Damnations', the letter articulated these concerns, pointing out that '. . . the points situation has reached a ridiculous level' and '. . . in a branch as small as mine, is it fair to have 33% of Chief Petty Officers on 2OE as well as others on extended service . . . this must surely have an adverse effect on promotion'.

Navy News is effectively part of the management structure of the Navy, supplying a relentlessly positive upbeat picture of the Service to the RN itself and the public. Remarkably, it published this anonymous dissenting letter, indicating that management deemed it necessary to reply. Captain W.J. Davis of the MoD replied, 'the roster to POA(Phot) is certainly longer than the management would wish' and cited complex reasons. He explicitly denied that 2OE had caused problems, '. . . since its inception 2OE has been blamed for all manner of ills, most of which are not attributable'. He concluded, 'Promotion prospects are given full consideration with allocation quotas, and every effort is made, particularly with the smaller branches, to ensure acceptable career factors are maintained'.

Despite this reassurance, in practice the delay became over ten years for most, and became a great source of amusement to the rest of the fleet. Sadly, this humour was lost on the 35–40-year-old Leading Hands who were required to serve on ships living in Junior rates mess-decks with 17-year-olds, while their peers and friends from source branches were Petty Officers and Chief Petty Officers, commensurate with their age and experience. The anonymous letter writer also commented on this disparity, '. . . an annoying factor . . . is the constant explanations I find myself giving both at sea and ashore with reference to my senior years and junior status. It becomes increasingly embarrassing trying to justify to other ranks the reasons behind slowness in promotion . . . the lengthy wait is steadily eroding my enthusiasm'.

Many ratings of great ability and experience were lost to the Service due to this perceived problem with promotion, which in fairness must be stated to have existed for many years since the late 1940s. CPO(Phot) Paul Yockney recalls, 'Senior ratings who, despite being well past their sell-by date, [are] allowed to cling on for year after year whilst, at the same time, killing the ambition of the younger ratings. I can well remember in the mid-1970s at Culdrose several good LA(Phot)s who left the Service because the future was nothing less than bleak'. It may be convincingly argued that these demographic problems forced many to leave, contributing greatly to the general sense of apathy that became prevalent in certain areas into the 1990s and indeed beyond. Even today, further Branch reductions, (to be detailed later) are having the same effect and bode ill for the future, as those with any

Right:
Returning from the Outback '88 exercise, the three aircraft-carriers of the Royal Navy (HMS *Invincible*, *Illustrious* and *Ark Royal*) were steamed together off Portland for the benefit of the assembled barrage of cameras and film-makers. Pictures like this are often used for political purposes – careless reproduction of this image without qualification for the special circumstances under which it was taken could lead the public to deduce that Britain can afford to run three aircraft-carriers. The reality, of course, is considerably more prosaic – the Royal Navy does not now have enough personnel or aircraft to operate three carriers without detriment to other units.

Right:
The Gulf War provided photographers with the surreal background of burning oil-fields, torched by the Iraqi soldiers as a last gesture of hate when they withdrew from Kuwait. On 1 March 1991, the day after the war finished, PO(Phot) 'Al' Campbell was fortunate enough to obtain an air-to-air sortie over Kuwait with a Sea King of 845 NAS and the Lynx helo from HMS *Brave*. This amazing sortie produced several highly original images, demonstrating yet again that there is no substitute for the experienced RN photographer on the scene.

'get up and go' literally do get up and go – outside the Royal Navy.

These problems were further exacerbated by an arbitrary drafting policy and divisive professional arguments that began to affect the Branch as a whole. Certain ratings were preferentially allowed to serve a considerable amount of their time in the Yeovil/Portland 'circuit', or at RNAS Culdrose. This was, of course, not consistent with drafting policy and deprived others of the opportunity to serve in these areas. Strong internal divisions grew within the Branch and were allowed to flourish as no firm action was taken. These divisions were fuelled by certain photographic sections, primarily Director Public Relations (Navy) DPR(N) in London, where certain individuals caused much offence by broadcasting the humorous supposition that they were better photographers than the ship/unit that they had been temporarily detached to – a delusion perhaps fuelled by the fact that they wore suits whilst employed in London and cultivated an air of 'exclusivity' to normal members of the Branch.

Finally, some Senior Ratings assumed disproportionally powerful positions, once again primarily by longevity and tolerated without censure. These factors contributed to a strong feeling of resentment in the Branch as a whole. It was no accident that the annual Peregrine Trophy social event was known as the 'Backstabber's Ball', notorious for the bad feeling and sniping comments that accompanied the individual competition entries and certain 'cliques' of the attendees.

Despite these serious policy flaws, the daily work of the Branch continued apace. During the Gulf Conflict of 1991, photographers were deployed to good effect, using the recently purchased Hasselblad transmitters to rapidly send pictures to the Press Association. PO(Phot) Alastair Campbell, of Falklands fame, again produced classic work for the world's media; his stunning helicopter and burning oil-well photographs remain some of the most memorable images of the entire Royal Navy effort. Operation *Haven*, the ill-fated attempt to help the abandoned Kurds after the Gulf War, was covered by PO(Phot) 'Jan' Brayley with the Royal Marines and LA(Phot) Wilkinson, attached to 846 Naval Air Squadron, producing harrowing images of this tragic situation that were hardly used.

The exercise Orient '92 provided opportunities for HMS *Invincible* and a host of smaller ships, while the ice-patrol ship HMS *Endurance* (always a popular draft) continued her uninterrupted cycle of deployments to Antarctica. The assault ship HMS *Fearless*, amazingly still in service despite her age, carried one photographer, but often more when embarking for exercises.

Behind the scenes, the insidious advent of budgeting began to be seriously felt within the Branch. Suddenly, the accounting required for budgeting began to quantify, in exact amounts of money, exactly what each photographic section was doing and how much it cost each Commanding Officer or Higher Level Budget Holder. This resulted in a large scale rationalisation, epitomised by the predicament of the budget holder at HMS *Dolphin*, who could either keep his photographer or his Physical Training Instructor (PTI). There is still physical training at HMS *Dolphin*. Ridiculous out-of-branch drafts, such as the Commander's Assistant's Assistant at HMS *Dryad* (walking the Commander's dog, running the 'tea-boat', reading the newspapers and never touching a camera) were sensibly disposed of. Most small sections and single billet drafts were rapidly decimated, concentrating facilities in larger units, but even then the hunger of the budget holders was not satisfied. The very existence of the Branch was repeatedly questioned and several large sections were condemned, then reprieved when individual Commanding Officers objected. Rumour and counter-rumour circulated, driven by the nagging doubt that a cohesive and reasoned front was not being presented to the very real threat that existed.

The Fleet Photographic Unit at Tipner changed 'owner' and name again in March 1992, renamed the Surface Flotilla Photographic Unit (SFPU) and now under the new accounting authority of Flag Officer Surface Flotilla (FOSF). Some new practices were introduced in an attempt to improve the image of the Branch and several high profile deployments by staff from the unit were a great success. In particular, the fiftieth anniversary of D-Day in 1994 was a busy day for the unit. It was photographed well, unobtrusively and produced excellent images which were disseminated worldwide.

Photographers were also loaned from SFPU to augment permanent staff on the two aircraft carriers, who had the demoralising and ultimately

Above:
Continuing the memorable sortie over the newly-liberated Kuwait, the famous towers of the capital provide an impressive backdrop for the two aircraft.

Below:
The misguided American and British attempts to incite the Kurds to rebellion after the Gulf War have left a legacy of shame and further genocide. On 24 April 1991, the Royal Marines were sent on the humanitarian Operation *Haven* to resupply the refugees. 'Al' Campbell took this public relations shot, perhaps showing where the Allied push into Iraq should have ended.

Above:
During 1993, HMS *Invincible*'s stand off visit to Corfu after Adriatic duties was cut short by the need to host peace talks on board. All three factions in the civil war needed somewhere mutually acceptable to meet, where there was a reduced risk of kidnapping, assassination or other unpleasantness indelibly associated with these players. HMS *Invincible*'s wardroom was therefore converted to a conference room, and the factions arrived in independent helicopters – not photographed on board by order despite departures to the ship being featured on 'Sky' news. David Owen and the UN's special ambassador, Stoltenberg, tried all day to resolve the conundrum that is Bosnia, with little success. After much pressure a record photograph was permitted, and LA(Phot)s 'Wolfie' Wilkinson and Mick Storey were briefly allowed in to take the shot. After a very short period they were sent out, but not before 'Wolfie' had taken this impressive picture of Radovan Karadic, who was clearly very uncomfortable with being photographed. This man is now recognised in his true colours, as an international war criminal whose barbarism and misguided Serbian imperialism has been responsible for the greatest outbreak of suffering in Europe since Hitler.

Above right:
This photograph demonstrates the key hallmark of a naval photographer, the ability to produce a good result from the apparently mundane. PO(Phot) Kev Preece caught the four Sea Kings of 845 Naval Air Squadron approaching their new base in Split, Bosnia, reflected low over the sullen waters of the Adriatic in 1993.

Right:
Early reconnaissance pictures taken by the Sea Harriers of 800 NAS over parts of Bosnia confirmed the dreadful reports of ethnic cleansing and worse. This shot from 1993 clearly shows the characteristic destruction of individual houses in a small village, whilst others remain completely intact – probably occupied by their murderers.

purposeless task of rotating as six-monthly duty in the Adriatic in support of the United Nations in Bosnia, impotently circling whilst the horror continued inland. Processing reconnaissance on board the carrier was again an essential task, expedited for early analysis, although shortages of RN Photo Interpretation staff forced the loan of an experienced RAF Flight Sergeant in the early stages. However, the decision by HMS *Invincible*'s senior air staff to continuously video-record Sea Harrier operations by day and night (on a commercial camera completely unsuited to the task), failed over a three-year period to record any footage of anything more interesting than an engine 'pop' surge and proved hugely demoralising. Changes in humidity between the inside and outside of HMS *Invincible* regularly caused the video camera to shut itself down, a serious limitation frequently represented up the chain of command without resolution. It was, therefore, no coincidence that both Sea Harrier aircraft lost close to the carrier between 1993–6 were not captured on video. This tasking was certainly instrumental in persuading some of the ultimate futility of informed photographic representation.

Royal Navy photographers also served with 845 Naval Air Squadron, based in Split and in Sarajevo during the bitter civil war that tore Bosnia apart. On several occasions these ratings were on hand to witness and record evidence of the medieval and barbaric atrocities discovered. Some of these images are now being used by the International Tribunal, set up to apprehend and convict war criminals from that tragic country.

THE FUTURE

At the time this history is being written, the Photographic Branch survives tenuously, clinging to life in an environment at least as hostile as the early 1990s. It has barely survived a concerted attempt to disprove its viability, the Director of Naval Manpower 'Major Management Study' of April 1996 (produced after cursory inspection visits and a deep concern for statistics and percentages). The Branch has been savagely pruned as a result of the study, with a target of 75 people to be met by March 1998. As there are still too many photographers in the Branch, fourteen fully-trained ratings will be moved by this date to jobs anywhere in the Navy, non-photographically employed in driving or security work – little reward for those who have sacrificed promotion prospects and time to join an elite professional 'career'. The management euphemism for this change is 'de-enrichment', deemed necessary to rationalise the RN photographic tasks. Middle management are collectively impotent to act, as the decisions are being taken by the real power in today's Royal Navy – the budget holders.

A key wind change can be detected by the recategorisation of the Branch, from a 'branch' with implicit career structures, implications and roles, to a 'specialisation' which is much easier to attack and contractualise piece by piece. This change appears mere semantics, but is in fact a clear indication that the perceived importance of the Branch to the upper echelons of power is being degraded. Equally, the Branch is experiencing difficulty gaining access to these decision-makers, as historically the Royal Navy's higher structures are drawn from sea-going command. In the past, these Commanders and Captains met and saw the ship's photographers at work, whereas today the severely limited opportunities for sea service make these contacts more difficult to sustain. An example of this liaison in the 1960s was Lt-Cdr 'Ron' Daplyn RN, who knew Commander-in-Chief Naval Home Command personally after flying with him in the War. Any problems were swiftly resolved after a visit to see the Admiral.

However, despite these political machinations, and as can be expected from a Branch of professionals, excellent work continues to flow from the sections left after the cull. Some sections with clear operational tasking, such as HMS *Neptune*, which supports the Faslane submarine base in Scotland, have substantially progressed and are good examples of the way the Branch can be made viable in the 1990s.

The famous Lt-Cdr Gordon Ford RN, who himself rose from the lower deck after a period of distinguished service, particularly on HMS *Britannia*, has fought valiantly at DGS(LE) for the Branch to be well equipped. A particular success was the £200,000 allocated for the procurement of Digital Photographic Equipment (DPE). They are now in use with deploying RN photographers, giving a rapid means to send images to the new central data bank at the Surface Flotilla Photographic Unit. Proving the value of this system is the response of LA(Phot) Wilkinson, deployed on HMS *Liverpool* at the 1997 volcanic eruption at Monserrat, from where imagery has been sent daily around the world, published in newspapers as diverse as the *International Herald Tribune* and the *Daily Telegraph*.

However, the RN image bank concept needs much work before it reflects a comparable civilian effort and a substantial move in the right direction would be the recognition (by the officers at the SFPU) of the amount of work required and the appropriate allocation of manpower. The expensive Nikon F5 camera system has also been purchased by DGS(LE), although many in the Service were surprised at this choice, as the Nikon F90 has been

Below:
The number of WRNS in the Branch has now fallen dramatically, as reduced recruiting and the departure of many senior women takes a toll on numbers. Wrens who transferred to the Branch by sideways entry in the late 1980s were given the option of sea service, in common with other branches. Very few actually took up the challenge, but those who did have proved popular additions on board HMS *Invincible* and HMS *Fearless*. Unfortunately, those who demonstrated initiative and went to sea were placed on the men's promotion roster (i.e. no chance), while the WRNS who remained shoreside stayed on a much smaller roster and therefore achieved promotion far more quickly. This manifest unfairness, and the typical failure of the RN to deal with it, has caused the regretable early loss of some of the best Wren ratings.

Above:
Pictures of the volcanic eruption on Monserrat were sent by Apple Mac computer direct from HMS *Liverpool* to DPR(N) in London, pushed out to national papers the same day and appeared in major broadsheet newspapers across the world. Pictures of this kind are of great value in showing the public that the Royal Navy is on the spot, raising public awareness about how their defence money is spent.

Below:
There is still a clear role for the Photographic Branch in the Royal Navy of the future, if those budget holders responsible can be persuaded. In the meantime, work continues apace in what remains of the fleet. Phot staff on board HMS *Invincible* in the Adriatic photograph 814 Naval Air Squadron aircrew, dressed for exercise in NBC clothing.

extensively tested by Petty Officer's Qualifying Courses under the instruction of CPO(Phot) Alan Ferguson in the early 1990s and is considerably more robust.

Several policy issues still need to be addressed by the British close to home, including the decaying and damaged Royal Navy archive, but overall significant efforts have been made to improve the Branch's image. Facilities are to be centralised in Regional Processing Centres (RPCs), complemented with a pool of Service photographers and civilian assistants (TG2 status) and tasked to provide an efficient and effective processing facility for all units within its geographical area. Encouragingly, despite the depredations of poor promotion and budget holders, a reasonable number of ratings remain whose enthusiasm and dedication rise above the regrettable political machinations.

It is fair to say that many old photographic requirements have gone for ever, replaced by a combination of technology and machinery. An Apple Mac computer outputting to a Canon photocopier can do more work than five photographers, while the Gretag film processing machines at the Surface Fleet Photographic Unit are identical to those used by Tesco in Portsmouth. However, the Branch still has an important role to play, particularly in the sea-going field, and it can only be hoped that some enlightened Higher Level Budget Holder can be persuaded of this. It cannot have escaped notice that the Branch could actually pay for itself by selling images, perhaps to picture libraries or sub-contracted out. It is arguable that only by opening minds to new practices and approaches will the Branch survive. Perhaps the drafting of some Chief Petty Officers to sea would counter the Branch's prevalent reputation in the fleet; representing the specialisation on the front line rather than the office, where the battle is certainly being lost.

After the issue of DCI RN 25/97, the Branch now has clearly defined and prioritised tasks which must be adhered to for the chance of survival. These rationalisation changes have now been endorsed and ratified by the Sub Navy Board, and have been redefined into primary and secondary areas as follows:

Primary tasks	Operational – naval collection of intelligence
	Image analysis
	Air reconnaissance
	Royal Marine operations
	Other – public relations
Secondary tasks	Weapons firings/trials
	Periscope calibration
	Additional qualifications for non-specialists
	Incident and accident reports
	Technical and defect reports
	Sailing directions and photogrammetry surveys
	Recognition
	Presentation materials
	Training support

Apparently obvious steps in command and control of such a specialist branch are now beginning to be taken, but the maintenance of a central image file and accurately catalogued archives still need addressing. These steps alone would significantly enhance the perception of the specialisation and give the appearance of a regulated, cohesive approach to defending its existence. Half thought-out plans, or even worse, half executed, are a major contributory factor to the fleet-wide impression of disorganisation and apathy that exists at present.

Another factor of concern should be the diminished perception of the modern Branch in what remains of the 'General Service' fleet of the Royal Navy. There is an underlying opinion that photographers are out to enrich themselves, with no understanding of the important work undertaken by the Branch. This widespread ignorance is demonstrated not only by those in command, whose requirement for immediacy despite quality erodes a professional ethos, but by the lower deck whose perception of the Branch is poor. Even markedly talented individuals, such as Chris North, 'Fez' Parker or 'Dizzy' de Silva, whose worth would be recognised in any comparable civilian institution, experience major difficulties in organising anything more than a group photograph.

This ludicrous situation is further exacerbated by the free assistance given to any civilian organisation invited by the 'proactive' PR staff on to ships or submarines. Instantly afforded every convenience, including air assets, these individuals and agencies often achieve more in a week than ship's photographers do in a deployment. This problem, like so many outlined in these pages, has historical precedent. A photographer on board HMS *Centaur* in 1965 states, '. . . I obtained some unusual pictures of deck operations from the ship's SAR Whirlwind, hovering very close to the top of the ship's mast and in formation with the "plane guard" during (jet) recovery because, quite simply, I was sat alongside a *Sunday Times* photographer who was given the run of the ship for a week whilst we were in the Mediterranean'. Perhaps this situation is partially the fault of the Branch, which has signally failed to make the fleet aware of its capabilities.

The General Service and budget holders would do well to remember the benefits of in-house photographers. When a warship collides with another, criminal investigations of sexual assaults take place or suicides occur on ships, the Photographic Branch is there; widely experienced, professional and most importantly from the public relations/media point of view, under the direct military command and control of the Senior Officer or task originator. The author awaits with some amusement the vain efforts that the Royal Navy will take, attempting to contain or 'damage limit' some of the more unpleasant situations that occur at sea, once contract or civilian photographers become involved. The Royal Navy's highly-paid public relations staff clearly know better, as they not only allowed the 1994 HMS *Brilliant* television series to be made and transmitted, but actively supported it as good public relations. The appalling scenes of sexist abuse to the ship's contingent of WRNS, the men dressed in women's clothing going ashore (over the gangway) and other outrageous behaviour prompted the Commander on board HMS *Invincible* in 1994 to point out that this kind of behaviour would never be tolerated on his ship.

Internal circulation RN publications and public relations outlets also have a role to play in the survival of the Branch, as they could acknowledge in a prominent manner the support they receive from RN Service photography. Classic examples of this are the RN *Broadsheet* annual periodical and the excellent Fleet Air Arm *Flight Deck* magazine, both of which always credit naval photographers and often carry express indications that they rely heavily on this imagery. This acknowledgment sharply contrasts with the editorial policy of the self-styled 'Newspaper of the Royal Navy' – *Navy News*, which exists in a niche market due to a captive audience and no outside competition. Arbitrarily crediting RN photographers with no logical basis, despite protestations to the contrary, the failure to highlight the largest single source of their pictures (and indeed, their success as a 'newspaper') was still resulting in exchanges of letters between Photographic Officers at the SFPU and the Editor in 1996. *Navy News* has received many awards for its use of Branch produced pictures; it would therefore be appropriate for it to play a more prominent role in the matter of acknowledgment before its pictures are permanently supplied by the gifted amateurs that grace their pages with some monotony.

Peripheral evidence, casting light on the strain of this unattractive employment situation, is the damage inflicted on the most important and ignored single factor in this equation – the RN Photographic staff themselves. Job satisfaction, the most commonly cited reason for transfer to the Branch, is approaching new lows, compounded by negligible promotion prospects, doubts about Branch viability and the sure knowledge that by precedent the Royal Navy does not make people redundant from small branches – it cynically forces them out. It is no coincidence that the Photographic Branch has the shameful stigma of the highest divorce rate per specialisation in the RN – 75% over the last fifteen years.

CONCLUSIONS

To present a balanced picture, the disapassionate criticisms outlined must be set in context against the privileged position of those fortunate enough to serve in the Branch. Occupying a unique position in the RN, based on the 'lower deck' but with regular access to the highest echelons of power, the Royal Navy photographic trade was, and occasionally still is, the best professional task in the Service without exception. Well equipped for the task, and allowed a degree of personal autonomy and initiative seldom experienced elsewhere, only the most pedestrian of ratings have failed to appreciate the opportunities available. Keen ratings could achieve photographically beyond any dreams they might have had in training, vindicating the uncertain path to the specialisation and the long wait for promotion. The author is permanently grateful for the opportunity of serving in such a dynamic Branch and has attempted to create a sympathetic but accurate portrait through empirical observation and research.

Below:
The author records a Sea Harrier FA2 launch from the goalkeeper position alongside the ramp, on HMS *Invincible*, 1994.

The Photographic Branch clearly remains a viable proposition to the Royal Navy of today and tomorrow, possessing the equipment and people to provide a high-quality service. The enormous untapped commercial potential of RN imagery requires detailed examination, as it may prove to be the most persuasive justification to the budget holders for retention of the Branch. It is clearly a paradox for the taxpayer to be paying for over one hundred photographers whose work is rarely seen outside a small 'circuit'. This situation was unwittingly confirmed by the Editor of *Navy News* in the illuminating foreword to his fascinating *Navy in the News 1954–1991* publication (HMSO) '. . . Many of the pictures [in the book] are unique . . . specially commissioned from the Royal Navy's own Photographic Branch . . . they have appeared nowhere else but on the pages of *Navy News*'.

The enormous effort generated every year by the annual Peregrine Trophy, which has matured into a showcase of sorts for the Branch, could be harnessed by allowing more prestigious civilian institutions, such as the British Institute of Professional Photography and the Royal Photographic Society, to view and borrow the display boards, in addition to the 'FOCUS' exhibition already attended each year. At present the prints from previous years lie discarded and uncared for in the old cine studio at Tipner. However, a recent positive move is the initiative by PO(Phot) de Silva to put the Trophy results, rules and a history of the Branch on the Internet, raising the profile and awareness of naval photography worldwide – these may now be located at *http://www.royal-navy.mod.uk/new/latest/pereg/hello.html*. There are also details of the Naval Photographer's Association on this web site, an organisation established in 1993 by the popular Lt Ian 'Shiner' Wrightson to provide some sort of continuity and support network for ex-naval photographers. The aims of the Association are to provide regular meetings on a social and professional basis, to produce a regular newsletter, to act as a point-of-contact through the Secretary and to produce a History of the Branch suitable for future reference. At inception, the Peregrine Trophy was

Above:
In the seventy-eight-year period of this history, the Royal Navy Photographic Branch has intermittently occupied the isolated plot at Tipner. Beginning with the RNSOP and now housing the single biggest section that remains, the site has seen many changes and formed an unforgettable part, for good and bad, in thousands of lives. Rumours persist that the unit will be relocated, forced by the imminent sale of the land, but the day-to-day photographic work continues unabated. Several of the original buildings remain, including the Film Studio, abandoned after the construction of the M275 motorway in 1975–76 introduced permanent noise levels that precluded film production – this shot provides an interesting comparison with the 1939–41 aerial shot previously reproduced on page 17.

intended to form a focal point, allowing members and ex-members to gather together at a social event to view the prints and meet old acquaintances. Possible resurrection would produce a little more Branch cohesiveness than is demonstrated at present.

Attachment at a senior level to an officer of Flag Rank, possibly associated with public relations, would also help the Branch immeasurably, ensuring a high public profile could be maintained and allowing the best use of assets. Finally, a determined effort from those who are charged with the stewardship of this tiny Branch would be most welcome. A vigorous effort to raise its profile could easily be made, as it urgently needs protecting from further cuts.

At present, the progressively deeper financial budget constraints inflicted on the Royal Navy, which will only get worse after the next expected Defence Review, mean that when Commanding Officers are faced with the stark choice of security ratings or photographers, necessity must prevail. The reality of rationalisation is that the Branch is being ground down, to levels below which it cannot hope to provide a service. It is unfortunate to leave the history of this amazing Branch on this note, but objectivity is infinitely preferable to subjective prevarication.

However, the Branch has always been threatened with closure, yet continues to labour on whilst rumour and counter-rumour circulate. Indeed, as 1999 dawns, the situation outlined in preceding pages may yet change – the Major Management Study of 1996 has been recognised as unrealistic and flawed, and the bitter resistance to cutbacks put up by Senior Rates in almost every section is finally being heeded. It is one thing to cut an air station's or submarine base's photographic services on paper, but more difficult when courageous Senior Rates inform Flag Officers directly of the real effect at 'street level'. In a career system which favours the sycophant over the individualist, personal initiative and straight talking still have a role to play. Unless a more spirited and aggressive rearguard action is fought, the Branch may already be lost as the thread supporting the sword of Damocles frays still further. It will be a sad end to a Branch with such a proud history. At present, the future is too uncertain to predict.

POSTSCRIPT and UPDATE

Discerning readers will have noted that a particular area of concern outlined in the text was the condition of the negative archives in the vaults at Tipner, which contained material of priceless historical value including the entire collection of H.M. Yacht *Britannia*. Fortunately, the decision was taken (entirely separate of the sentiments expressed in this manuscript) early in 1998 to transfer the entire archive to more appropriate surroundings, these being the Imperial War Museum for the Naval material and the Royal Archive at Windsor Castle for the *Britannia* collection. Those with the history of the Branch at heart will view this as a most welcome step, particularly in the light of the inadequate supervision previously exercised, and it is indeed fortuitous that 'current Naval legislation' (as stated by the head of the Branch, Lt-Cdr T. Hogan R.N. in letter 13.01.98) has provided for the security of this archive just as this book goes to print.

Confirmation of the importance of this archive was supplied in dramatic fashion by *The Sunday Times Magazine* of 19 April 1998, which featured fifteen pages of exclusive Royal Navy photographs of royalty on board H.M. Yacht *Britannia*, spanning a forty-year period. Journalist Michael Bilton, who wrote the newspaper article accompanying the story, described the *Britannia* archive as 'a genuine historical treasure trove of national importance', and went on to say; 'life holds few real surprises, but the size and quality of the *Britannia* photographic archives is one of them'. Quantifying the *Britannia* part of the archive at one hundred thousand images, the article further discussed the main Naval archive; 'In December, the decision was made to relocate the archive of almost one million photographs . . . . the vast bulk will be kept by the Imperial War Museum'. The process of transferring the negatives to the I.W.M. and Windsor Castle has now begun, closing the chapter on the archives at Tipner in a most positive way.

This book was cleared for publication at the end of March 1998, requiring a few minor alterations. In particular, the Ministry of Defence required an explicit disclaimer for some of the opinions expressed in the later pages of this manuscript, stating; 'the section entitled The Future does seem to be something of an impassioned plea for the survival of the . . . . Branch . . . . which, in part, is quite damning and is of course subjective'. This disclaimer now appears at the front of this book, but it is hoped that the reader may appreciate that the author has attempted to produce an historically accurate document irrelevant of what 'should' be – reflecting what actually occurred instead of a sanitised and therefore less accurate account. Voltaire suggested; 'he who ventures to write contemporary history must expect to be criticised both for everything he has said and everything he has not said'. All quotes and information in this publication have been obtained through exhaustive research and interviews – the historical material for this book will be deposited with the archives of the Naval Photographers Association on completion.

COLOUR PORTFOLIO 1985–1998

Above:
100th Anniversary of Tower Bridge, London
('Dizzy' de Silva, 1994)

Following page:
HMS *Cardiff* leaves Gibraltar
(Richie Moss, 1995)

Previous page:
HMS *Invincible* breaks from HMS *Ark Royal*
(Neil Mercer, 1994)

Right:
HMS *Active* fires saluting guns when
entering Kiel (Richie Moss, 1994)

Below:
HMS *Invincible* in the Indian Ocean,
returning from Orient '92 (Dave Trish, 1992)

Left:
NATO Standing Force Mediterranean off
Mount Carmel, Haifa (Flo Ford, 1994)

Below:
Training in a Damage Control simulator
(Steve Saywell, 1995)

Right:
HMS *Invincible* hands over to HMS
Illustrious in Gibraltar (Artie Shaw, 1995)

Below:
MCM flotilla leaves Rosyth for the last time
('Dizzy' de Silva, 1995)

Above:
Lynx helicopter recovers to Type 22 ('Wolfie' Wilkinson, 1992)

Below:
HMS *Manchester* in heavy seas during the Global '86 deployment
(Les Warr, 1986)

Above:
NATO Standing Force Atlantic with a Seahawk helicopter
(Chris North, 1996)

Below:
HMS *Argonaut* hulk burns during SINKEX (weapons trials)
(Chris North, 1992)

Above:
HMS *Boxer* in the Indian Ocean ('Fez' Parker, 1992)

Below:
Bow of HMS *Lowestoft* as the ship sinks after weapons trials
(1986)

Above:
Last operational Seacat missile firing (Gary Davies, 1994)

Below:
Exocet firing on HMS *Brave* when she was acting as the West Indies guardship (Chris Brick, 1995)

Above:
HMS *Lowestoft* hit by torpedo from HMS *Conqueror* on weapons trials (1986)

Below:
Action stations (MacDonald, 1995)

Opposite:
HMS *Argyll* in Plymouth Sound for the VE-Day anniversary celebrations ('Iggy' Smith, 1995)

Left:
HMS *Exeter* visits Hong Kong (Eric Kennelly, 1996)

Below:
HMS *Invincible* returns to Portsmouth after her first Adriatic deployment (1994)

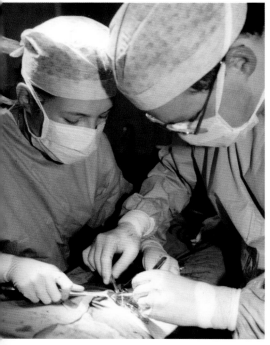

Above:
MA(Q) Tracey Barrett during operation on
HMS *Invincible* (Neil Mercer, 1995)

Above right:
Wren DSA Sue Beckett in Europa Point
lighthouse, Gibraltar (Chris North, 1987)

Right:
Wren during fire-fighting training
(Terry Seward, 1994)

Above:
HMS *Invincible* and F/S *Clemenceau* in the Adriatic Sea
(Neil Mercer, 1993)

Below:
Naval Special Forces Divers. September 1998.
(Steve Saywell)

![Naval Special Forces Divers]

Above:
Ship's diver of HMS *Atherstone* during mine clearance operations in the Gulf War, off Kuwait (Alastair Campbell, 1991)

Right:
'Old' HMS *Endurance* on patrol, seen through an iceberg (John Hicken, 1985)

Below:
Divers from HMS *Boxer* off Cyprus ('Fez' Parker, 1992)

Right:
'New' HMS *Endurance* on patrol (Craig Leask, 1993)

Above:
'Old' HMS *Endurance* alongside in Grytviken, South Georgia
('Dizzy' de Silva, 25 Dec 1989)

Below:
'New' HMS *Endurance* in pack ice, Weddell Sea, Antarctica
(Craig Leask, 1992)

Above:
Divers from HMS *Endurance* in ice, Antarctica (Stuart Warren, 1995)

Below:
'New' HMS *Endurance* ice-breaking (Stuart Warren, 1993)

Above:
'Old' HMS *Endurance* with Lynx survey
helicopters off Gibraltar (Chris North, 1989)

Left:
HM S/M *Trafalgar* outbound from Plymouth
on patrol ('Iggy' Smith, 1996)

Right:
The flag is lowered on HM S/M *Repulse* at sunset for the last time (Nathan Dua, 1996)

Below:
HM S/M *Courageous* proceeds on patrol from Faslane (Craig Leask, 1990)

Left:
H/M S/M *Trenchant* at the North Pole
(Andrew Chetty, 1994)

Below:
HMS *Marlborough* and HM S/M *Sceptre* off
the USA coast (Steve Saywell, 1996)

Above:
HM S/M *Unseen* head-on
(Craig Leask, 1990)

Right:
Submarine control panel and supervisor
(Jon Garthwaite, 1992)

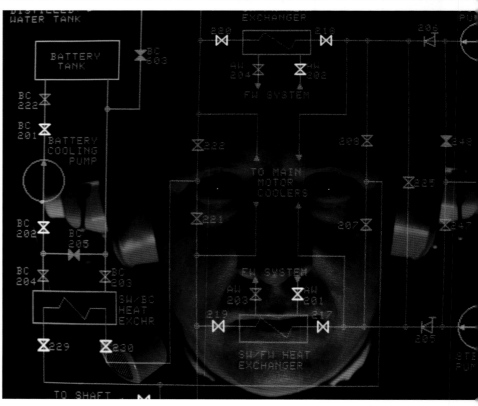

Left:
Commanding Officer training on periscope
(George Harvey, 1996)

Below:
'S' class submarine at high speed
Cumbraes, Scotland (Phil Ball, 1987)

Right:
Two 'R' class nuclear ballistic missile
'bomber' submarines in the Clyde
(Phil Ball, 1987)

Below:
'S' class submarine at speed
(Phil Ball, 1987)

Above:
Trident facility at Clyde nuclear submarine base, Scotland (Nathan Dua, 1995)

Below left:
HM S/M *Repulse* returns from her last ever Polaris patrol, Clyde submarine base (Alastair Campbell, 1996)

Below:
HM S/M *Resolution* proceeds on patrol from Faslane (Craig Leask, 1991)

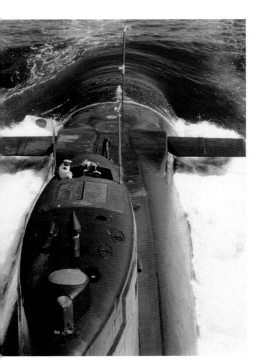

Right:
H/M Submarine *Sceptre* (Craig Leask, 1991)

Below:
Submarine escape trainer on HMS *Dolphin*
(Jon Garthwaite, 1991)

Above:
Cockpit shot with two Sea Harrier F/A2s on wingtips
(Neil Mercer, 1994)

Below:
845 NAS Sea King with burning oil-well, Kuwait
(Alastair Campbell, 1991)

Right:
Sea King helicopter of 845 NAS in Bosnia, May 1998. (Terry Seward)

Opposite above:
'The Sharks' Gazelle display team head-on (Steve Newbery, 1987)

Opposite below:
Sea Harrier FRS 1 with HMS *Ark Royal* (Neil Mercer, 1995)

Below:
Aircrew of 846 NAS. July 1998. (David Trish)

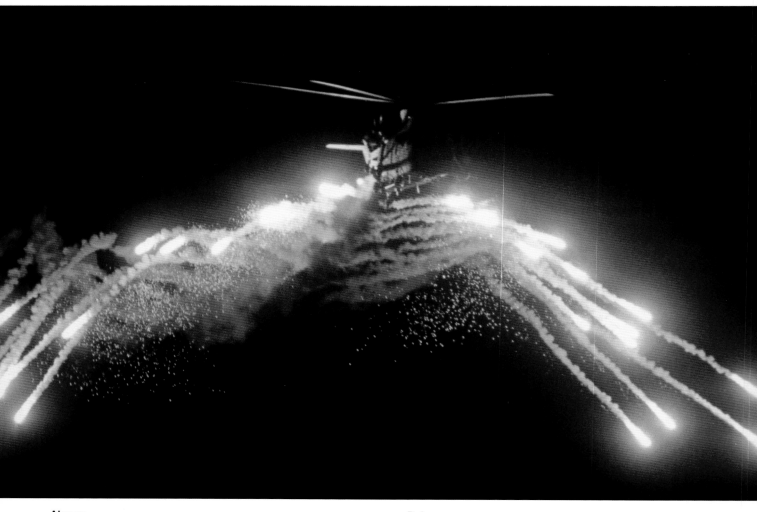

Above:
Sea King Mk 4 on flare test over Bosnia (Kevin Preece, 1993)

Below:
Seahawk's last flight before rebuild (Neil Mercer, 1989)

Above:
Gazelle display pair of 705 NAS (Bernie Pettersen, 1993)

Below:
845 NAS arrive in Kurdistan for Operation *Haven*
('Wolfie' Wilkinson, 1991)

Above:
Sea King of 771 NAS over St Michael's Mount, Cornwall
(N/K, 1996)

Below:
Lynx helicopter of HMS *York* escorts HMS *Illustrious* over Portland
Harbour (Chris North, 1988)

Above:
Sea King AEW pair over HMS *Invincible* in the Adriatic
(Neil Mercer, 1995)

Below:
Lynx helicopter reflected in the NEC building during a phot sortie,
Hong Kong ('Fez' Parker, 1992)

Above:
First live firing of Sidewinder AIM 9M missile from a Sea Harrier
(Kevin Preece, 1993)

Below:
High aspect Sidewinder firings during release trials for Sea Harrier
F/A2 (Neil Mercer, 1994)

Below:
Seven Sea Harrier FRS 1s in formation for
the 50th anniversary of 899 NAS
(Neil Mercer, 1992)

Above:
Gazelle of 705 NAS at RNAS Culdrose,
Cornwall (Ian Arthur, 1997)

Above:
Sea Harrier T4(N) on Bonfire night, RNAS
Yeovilton (Brian Jones, 1995)

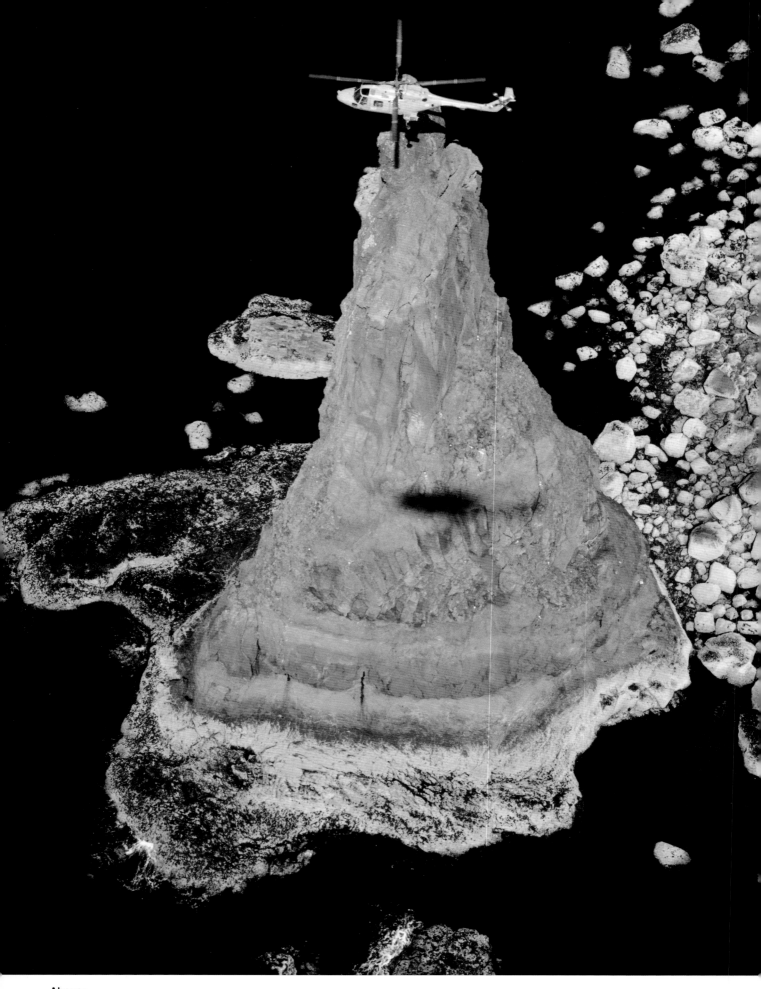

Above:
Lynx on rock pinnacle, Stornoway
('Dinger' Bell, 1992)

Left:
820 NAS Sea King conducts transfer with
HM S/M *Trenchant* (Chris North, 1990)

Below:
Lynx from HMS *Endurance* lands on
iceberg, Antarctica ('Dizzy' de Silva, 1989)

Above:
Lynx pair return from a sortie off Portland (Alan Ferguson, 1991)

Below:
814 NAS Sea King escorts a Kilo class submarine sold to the
Iranian Navy (Dave Trish, 1992)

Above:
Sea Harrier FRS 1 reflected in a pool of water on the deck of HMS *Ark Royal*
(Chris North, 1992)

Below:
Sea Harrier FRS 1 of 801 NAS in turn at sunset over Guernsey
(Neil Mercer, 1989)

Above:
Sea Harrier FRS1 reflected in a helmet visor
('Waggie' Wagstaff, 1989)

Above:
846 NAS Camouflaged Sea King over Norway
(Vincent Richards, 1990)

Below:
Wasp helicopter of 829 NAS fires an AS12 missile
(Chris North, 1987)

Left:
Cockpit view of the 'Sharks' Gazelle
helicopter display team
(Steve Newbery, 1986)

Below:
Sea King in the sea after running out of fuel
off Portugal
(Exercise Autumn Train) (N/K, 1985)

Opposite above:
Sea Harrier F/A2 of 899 NAS OEU over
RNAS Yeovilton (Neil Mercer, 1994)

Opposite below:
Sea Harrier T8 of 899 NAS with a Seahawk
(Dave Trish, 1997)

Above:
Hunter GA11 of FRADU loops through the
sun (Neil Mercer, 1990)

Opposite above:
Sea Heron communications aircraft over
Chesil Beach, Dorset (Nigel Thomas, 1986)

Opposite below:
Wasp helicopter over Portland
(Bill Butcher, 1986)

Right:
Lynx and Wasp helicopters in formation
during the change-over between the two
types (Chris North, 1986)

Below:
EH101 Merlin helicopter
(Alan Ferguson, 1991)

Right:
Lynx helicopter of 815 NAS over Lulworth Cove, Dorset (Chris North, 1986)

Right:
Sea King pair in Norway on a mountain flying exercise (Vincent Richards, 1990)

Right:
Sea King Mk 6 above clouds, showing cloud disturbance vortex (Ian Arthur, 1997)

Opposite above:
Sea Harrier FRS1s recover to HMS *Invincible* (Neil Mercer, 1994)

Opposite below:
Pair of 899 NAS Sea Harrier F/A2s over HMS *Invincible*
(Neil Mercer, 1994)

Above:
Russian carrier *Baku* reflected in the visor of
an aircrewman (Chris North, 1989)

Right:
Russian carrier *Baku* (1987)

Opposite:
'Yankee' class ballistic missile submarine
with HMS *Sheffield* (1991)

Above:
Russian 'Akula' class submarine reversing
into a smokescreen (1987)

Opposite above:
MiG 31 'Foxhound' Russian fighter aircraft
(Vincent Richards, 1988)

Opposite below:
Lynx helicopter with 'Slava' class Russian
warship from long-range (Alan Reid, 1988)

Above:
'Helix' contra-rotating helicopter in hover
over the sea (1988)

Opposite:
'Typhoon' class Russian nuclear ballistic
submarine (1989)

Above:
Dolphins playing around the bows of a
submarine during intelligence work
(Chris North, 1988)

Opposite above:
Royal Marines on exercise
(backlit by vehicle headlamps for effect)
(Neil Hall, 1995)

Opposite below:
Recce troop of 40 Cdo RM pickup on
exercise in Norway ('Dizzy' de Silva, 1992)

Above:
Royal Marines at the Edinburgh Military
Tattoo (Alastair Campbell, 1992)

Left:
Royal Marines boarding party in Lynx helo
(Chris North, 1994)

Opposite:
Royal Marines' patrol boat in Gareloch,
protecting the Clyde submarine base
(George Harvey, 1995)

Right:
Royal Marines firing mortars in Norway on
exercise ('Dizzy' de Silva, 1992)

Below:
Live GP machine-gun firings in the desert
('Dizzy' de Silva, 1991)

Above:
Royal Marines with artillery in Norway
('Dizzy' de Silva, 1992)

Opposite:
Live mortar firings in the desert for 42 Cdo
Royal Marines (James Gibson, 1994)

Left:
Royal Marines assault course training at
RMCTC Lympstone (Paul Cowpe, 1994)

Below:
Royal Marines trainee
(Dave McCormack, 1995)

Right:
Royal Marines patrol on exercise in woodland (Neil Hall, 1995)

Below:
Royal Marines patrol on exercise in Curacao ('Dizzy' de Silva, 1992)

Above:
HMY *Britannia* leads ships during D-Day
anniversary celebrations ('Fez' Parker, 1994)

Left:
HMY *Britannia* in dry dock at Portsmouth
during maintenance (Steve Lewis, 1996)

Opposite:
HMY *Britannia* flies the Royal Standard at sea (Andrew White, 1995)

Right:
HM the Queen with Prince Philip ('Dizzy' de Silva, 1996)

Below:
Fireworks over HMY *Britannia* in Sydney Harbour (Matt Wellings, 1988)

Below:
HMY *Britannia* enters Sydney Harbour
(Outback '88) (Matt Wellings, 1988)

Opposite:
Royal Marines detachment from HMS
Endurance on an iceberg
('Dizzy' de Silva, 1988)

Right:
PR shot of a sailor windsurfing in full uniform off Gibraltar (Chris North, 1990)

Below:
Royal Marines escaping from the Underwater Escape Training Unit ('Dizzy' de Silva, 1991)

Above:
Moslem child in Bosnia with mortar shell tail (Neil Mercer, 1994)

Above:
Child in a jungle village, Belize (Alastair Campbell, 1986)

Above:
Child in a jungle village, Belize (Alastair Campbell, 1986)

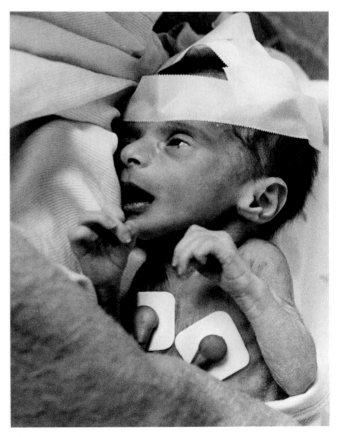

Above:
Orphan child dying in a Spanish military hospital, Kurdistan
(Brian Jones, 1986)

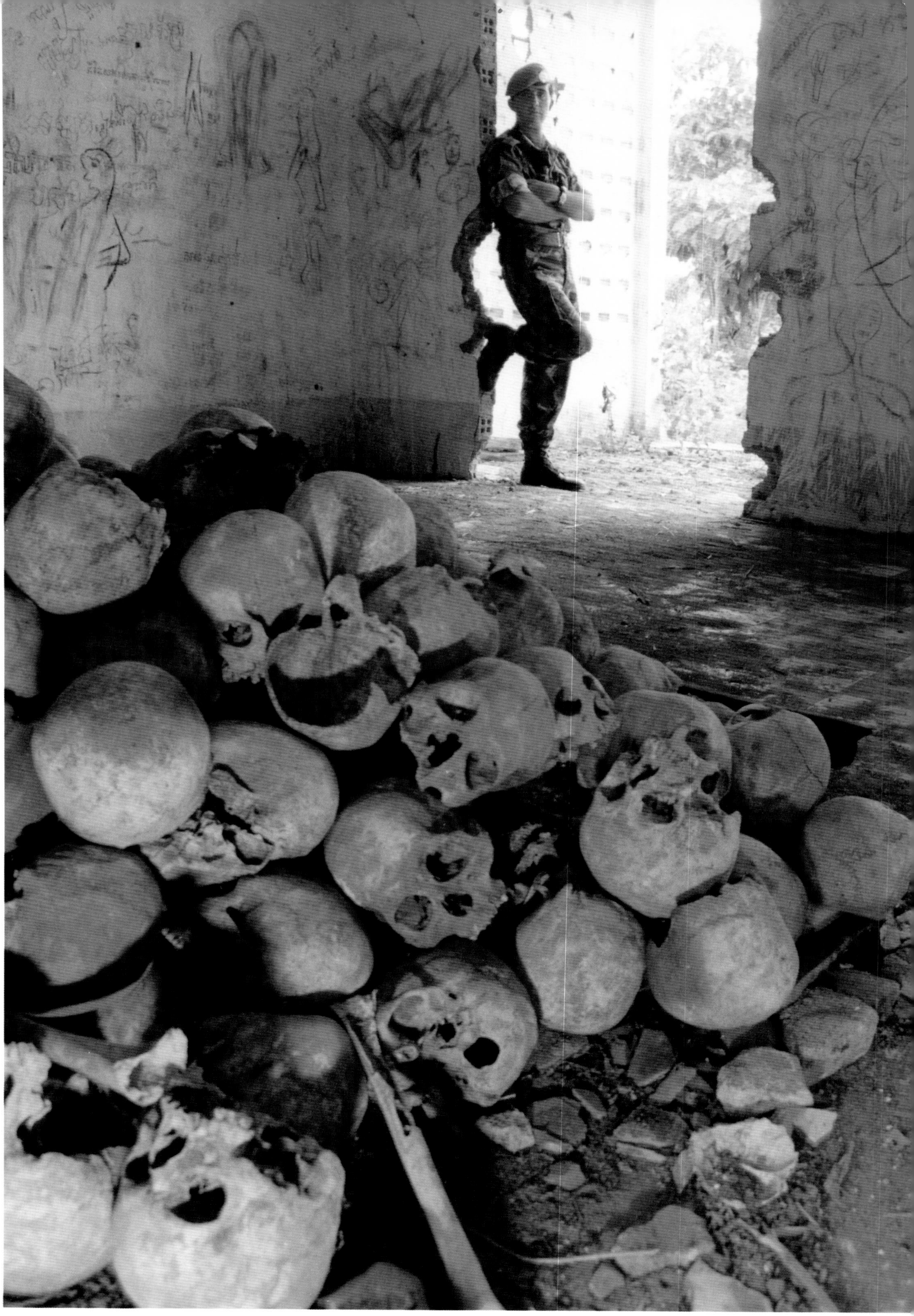

BIBLIOGRAPHY

Statement of Defence Estimates, 'Defending our Future', HMSO (1993)
Statement of Defence Estmates, 'A Sharp Sword in a Steady hand', HMSO (1994)
Statement of Defence Estimates, 'Stable Forces in a Strong Britain', HMSO (1995)
Annual Report Intelligence and Security Committee, HMSO (1996)
Central Intelligence Machinery, HMSO (1996)
Carrier Glorious, 'Life and Death of an Aircraft Carrier', Winton, Leo Cooper
Battleship, Middlebrook and Mahoney (Quoted by permission with thanks), Penguin (1987)
Soviet Sea Power in Northern Waters, Skogan/Brundtland, Pinter (1990)
The Hermes Adventure, Rex Morgan (Quoted by permission, with thanks), Runciman Press
Reminiscences of Naval Photography, Douglas Rendell, BJP (1980)
Unpublished research notes/papers/letters collected by Douglas Rendell
RN staff reports 1946 – AWD 1357/45
Admiralty Fleet Orders 1919/1921/1938 (various ADM series) PRO
Report of Proceedings Atlantic Fleet Spring Cruise 1920 (ADM/1/8586/68) PRO
Summary of Progress in Naval Gunnery 1914–36 PRO
Progress in Naval Gunnery 1925 (CB 981) PRO
Reconstitution of Naval Airman Branch absorbing Phots (ADM/1/21196) PRO
Navy Lists 1919–1944, Portsmouth/Plymouth Central Libraries
Royal Navy Book of Reference No. 870 1953 and 1993
Royal United Services Institute Journal 1937
Daily Mail reports October 1987 and 1996
Navy News, (1988 Ad Nauseum), Portsmouth Central Library
Memoirs Volume Three 'The Grand Alliance', Sir Winston Churchill
The Royal Navy Day by Day (2nd Edition), A.B. Sainsbury
Photographic Branch Newsletters, (1966, 1967, 1970, 1972, 1974), (Unpublished)
Flight Deck Fleet Air Arm magazine (1980 to date), Lt-Cdr Mike Caws RN (Ret'd)
RN Broadsheet Annual periodical (1987 to date), HMSO
Ships of the Royal Navy, J.J. College, Greenhill Books
The Royal Navy at Malta, Ellis and Warlow, Maritime Books
The Navy in the News 1954–1991, Allaway, HMSO
Royal Navy Language, John Hard, The Book Guild
Air Photography – Organisation and Training – AP 1354 HMSO (1936)
'Snaps', M. Critchley, Maritime Books (1986)
Defence Council Instructions Gen. 48/97 Open Government, MoD Internet site.
The Times Chronological Index – Plymouth Library
The Times 27 Feb 1985/23 July 1985 + *Sunday Times passim.*
Indiscretions of the Naval Censor. Rear-Adm. Sir Douglas Brownrigg Bt. Cassell 1920.
Aircraft Carriers, Norman Polmar. MacDonald London, 1969.
The War at Sea Vol 1. Capt. S. W. Roskill D.S.C., R.N. London 1954. H.M.S.O.
March to the South Atlantic. 42 Commando Royal Marines in the Falklands War. Nick Vaux.
No Picnic. 3 Commando Brigade, South Atlantic 1982. Julian Thompson. Leo Cooper 1985.
The Making of the Atomic Bomb, Richard Rhodes. Simon and Schuster (1986)
Hiroshima, John Hersey. Modern Library (1946)
Warships Illustrated No. 6 – The Soviet Navy Today, Milan Vego. Arms + Armour Press (1986)
Sovetskie Atomnye Podvodnye Lodki, V.V. Gagin Voronez (1995)
Bellona Report No. 2:96, Thomas Nilsen, Igor Kudrik and Alexandr Nikitin, incorporating photographs from *Rosvoorouzhenie*
Jane's Fighting Ships, 1980–1998, Portsmouth Central Library

Opposite:
RM officer with victims of the Kymer Rouge – Cambodia UN mission ('Fez' Parker, 1995)

Index